This book is to be returned on or before
the last date stamped below.

NEEDLEWORK ROOM 17/4/91

THE
TECHNIQUE OF
BATIK

THE
TECHNIQUE OF
BATIK

Noel Dyrenforth

B.T. BATSFORD LTD, LONDON

For my son, Jess

ISBN 0 7134 0407 8

Typeset by Servis Filmsetting Ltd, Manchester
and printed in Great Britain at
The Bath Press, Avon
for the publishers
B.T. Batsford Ltd
4 Fitzhardinge Street
London W1H 0AH

CONTENTS

Acknowledgements 7

Foreword 9

one
HISTORICAL BACKGROUND 11
Africa – China, Laos, Vietnam and Thailand – India – Japan – Machine wax printing

two
TRADITIONAL BATIK TECHNIQUES 25
Materials – Dyes and dyeing methods – Soga kerokan – Pekalongan method – Cap printing – Traditional patterns – Traditional garments

three
MODERN BATIK 45
The workshop – Fabrics – Preparation of fabrics – Wax – The wax pot – Tools – Colour and design

four
SYNTHETIC DYES 63
Dyes suitable for batik – General dye theory – Fibre-reactive dyes – Naphthol or azoic dyes – Vat dyes – Direct or application dyes – Acid dyes – Basic dyes – Discharge dyeing or bleaching – Steaming and fixing methods – Finishing

five
PROJECTS 75
1: combining techniques with creative responses
2: over-dyeing techniques with reactive dyes
3: wax removal between dyeing using naphthol or azoic dyes
4: direct dye application
5: stencilling
6: etching wax – sgraffito
7: wax printing

six
FURTHER EFFECTS WITH WAXING 125
Accidents will happen! – Technical variations to explore – Painting on silk using gutta resist techniques

seven
A GALLERY OF BATIK ARTISTS 133
Fritz Donart – Tony Dyer – Shigeki Fukomoto – Henk Mak – Miep Spée – Norma Starszakowna – Amri Yahya

CONVERSION TABLES OF WEIGHTS AND MEASURES 145

TEMPERATURE CONVERSION TABLE 145

GLOSSARY 147

LIST OF BATIK SUPPLIERS, ORGANIZATIONS, PERIODICALS, MUSEUMS, AND GALLERIES 151

BIBLIOGRAPHY 157

INDEX 159

FOREWORD

The intention of this book is to promote batik. It is also an invitation to probe into a fascinating dyeing process that can challenge and embellish the textile surface. The blending of a hot wax-resist, dye and cloth results in a unique and distinctive mode of expression. Coupled with skill and vision, batik has infinite potential for the artist.

I have concentrated on describing and illustrating a range of both traditional and modern techniques, from the use of waxing tools to the explicit documentation of dyes. Projects are devised to exploit materials and methods in a manner that will both stimulate and build up confidence.

I've also tried to impart some lessons and joys learnt from batik over the years. I trust, too, that the book will demonstrate the need for evaluation and progress. Batik is a valued medium that is not impervious to the opportunity of the widening art perspective.

1 Noel Dyrenforth demonstrating his craft.
'I first came upon batik in 1962 at an exhibition in Heals, London. I was stunned by the vibrant, crazily-marbled silk, although I didn't even know the name of the process then. Quickly attracted by the immediacy of the craft, I soon found a form of expression in batik which was liberating and exulting.'

ACKNOWLEDGEMENTS

I'm deeply grateful for all the support I've received in writing this book. I would particularly like to thank: Fiona Adamczewski, who gave professional advice and assistance with the text; Joël Degen, for his patient skills in providing the majority of the photographs; Tacy Long, for her faith; contributing batik artists, whose work I admire; and, not least, the students who, over the years, have badgered me into writing this all down.

NB. *Unless otherwise credited, all work shown is by the author.*

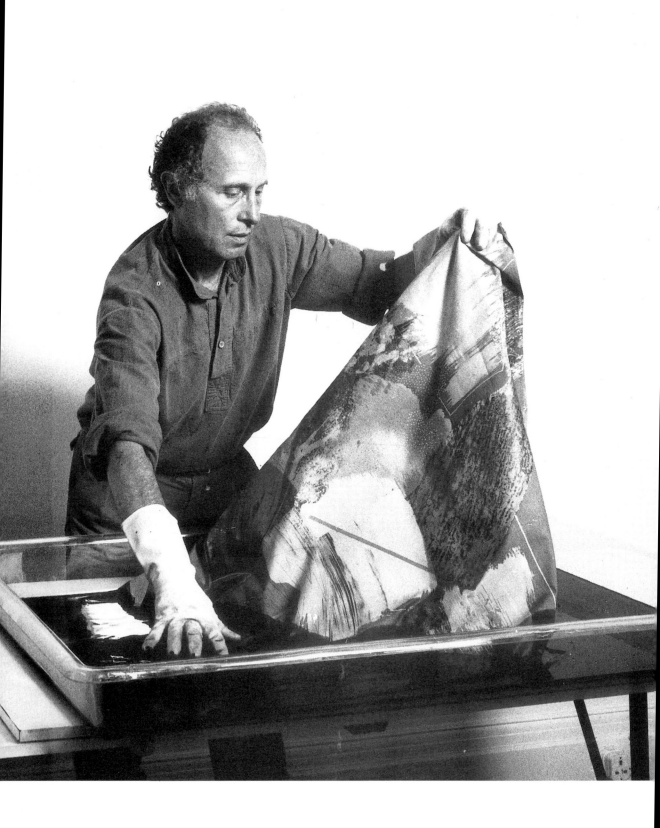

one

HISTORICAL BACKGROUND

The word *batik* is of Javanese origin. The verb *ambatik*, derived from *tik*, means to mark with spots or dots and, in a wider sense, signifies drawing, painting or writing. No such word is to be found in the old Javanese language, however, so we must conclude that batik is a word of fairly recent origin. It occurs for the first time in Dutch texts of the seventeenth century as a reference to a shipload of fabrics with coloured designs.

Batik is the word used to denote a particular method of applying coloured designs to fabric. This method involves covering certain sections of the design with a substance, usually liquid wax, so that they should retain the original colour of the fabric while it is subjected to the action of dyes. This substance, whether wax, rice paste or mud, is referred to as the *resist*. Fabrics thus treated may be monochrome or polychrome, depending upon the number of applications of wax and occasions when the fabric was subjected to the action of dyes.

The origins of batik are disputed by scholars. The earliest evidence has been found in four separate regions: the Far East, the Middle East, Central Asia and India. It is conceivable that these areas developed independently, without the influence from trade or cultural exchanges. However, it is more likely that the craft spread from Asia to the islands of the Malay Archipelago and west to the Middle East through the caravan routes. Of these early examples of batik, perhaps the most important collection is that preserved in the Shoso-in Repository of Imperial Treasures in Nara, Japan. These batiks are on silk and are in the form of screens. It is probable that they were made by Chinese artists, either working in their native China or as emigrants elsewhere, and they have been ascribed to the Nara period (AD 710–794). Japan was greatly influenced by the Sui and T'ang dynasties and these silk batiks are decorated with trees and animals, flute players, hunting scenes and stylized mountains.

Certainly, batik was practised in China as early as the Sui Dynasty (AD 581–618), and it is highly probable that silk batiks were exported to Japan, to Central Asia and, via the silk route, to the Middle East and India. In India the technique was transferred to cotton.

No evidence of very old batiks has yet been discovered in India, probably because of the nature of the climate which is not conducive to

2 Detail of a Pekalongan sarong by Eliza van Zuylen, c. 1920s.
Of the Dutch artists who adapted the native craft, Eliza van Zuylen ran a highly successful batik factory specializing in hand-drawn designs of mainly European character, memorable for their sharply defined arrangements of flowers and birds on pastel backgrounds with diagonal lines. She established her business in 1890, involving her whole family: the women concentrated on design and personnel and the men managed the dyeing and finance. The Second World War halted most batik production and she and her family were interned. Eliza van Zuylen died in 1947 aged 83. (Rudolf Smend Collection, Cologne)

3 Hand-drawn batik is called Tulis.

the conservation of fabrics, but frescoes in the Ajunta caves depict head-wraps and garments which could well have been batiks. Similarly, temple ruins in Java and Bali dating back to the thirteenth century contain figures whose garments are patterned in a manner suggestive of batik. By 1677, certainly, there is evidence that a considerable export trade to Java, Sumatra, Persia and Hindustan was in progress. Excavations conducted by Sir Aurel Stein in the Central Asian steppes of Sinkiang and Kansu provinces yielded examples of batik. Most of these were of silk, but one, decorated with blue and white motifs in cotton, has been identified as Indian. The silk clothes appear to originate, as do the screens of Nara, from China and are probably of the same period.

In Egypt, linen and, occasionally, woollen fabrics have been excavated, bearing white patterns on a blue ground. Although they have been used as shrouds, there is reason to believe that they originally served as hangings or altar covers in churches. These batiks, the oldest known, were made in Egypt and possibly also in Syria and date from the fifth century AD.

Indonesia, most particularly the island of Java, however, is the area where batik has reached the greatest peak of accomplishment. Initially, it was the pastime of privileged women of noble birth, but gradually it came to be the distinguishing mark of the dress of the aristocracy, and as its popularity increased, servants of aristocratic households and members of other sections of society were gradually involved in batik production. Finally, it came to be the national costume worn all over the islands. When the Dutch colonized Java, batik was introduced into Holland in the seventeenth century.

At first the designs were too exotic for popular taste, but early in the nineteenth century the Governor General of Java, Sir Thomas Raffles, published a history of batik. This aroused a great deal of interest and led to an intense study of the market potential, the methods and dyes em-

4 Spring by C. Bertram Hartman and Pieter Mijer
This batik made in 1919 was dip-dyed in eight different blues. The waxing was done entirely by brush. Pieter Mijer published the book Batiks and how to make them, *promoting the medium essentially as an art form. It had run to six editions by 1924.*

ployed and the possibility of developing machinery to produce imitations of batik prints that would be cheaper than hand-printed originals.

The English found it was not an easy matter to produce batik imitations on a large scale, nor imitate the richness of the originals. It was difficult to match the local vegetable dyes, and the patterns were of such complexity that an

5 Screen in Silk by Chris Lebeau
*From 1900, Lebeau was a leading designer from
the Haarlem School of Batik, popularizing the
medium amongst artists by his minute and
imaginative symmetrical designs featured mainly in
furniture inlays.*
(Royal Tropical Institute, Amsterdam)

enormous number of interlocking blocks and
rollers were required to reproduce them. This
made the cost prohibitive.

The Dutch, on the other hand, established a
factory at Leyden in 1835, and very rapidly other
factories followed at Rotterdam, Appledorn,
Helmand and Haarlem, where attempts were

made to produce batiks using the same techniques as those employed in Indonesia. Large numbers of Indonesian craftsmen were brought in and established in specially-built villages for the purpose of teaching the craft to Dutch workers. These Dutch workers, in turn, practised the craft in Holland before being transferred to the East Indies where they supervised the construction of state-controlled combines, uniting individual and family workshops.

In the early 1840s the Swiss had begun to export imitation batik sarongs, and at this point the Javanese workshops developed a form of wax block printing adapted from Indian techniques and known as *cap*, so that by the late 1870s the Swiss could no longer maintain the cost-effectiveness of their production.

By the early 1900s the Germans developed cantings made of glass, and electrically heated wax-writing devices with button-controlled spouts for the mass production of batiks. These methods were particularly effective in producing furnishing and curtaining fabrics, some of which retained areas of wax in a limited way so that they produced attractive semi-translucent effects.

In the general economic collapse of the 1920s the large-scale commercial production of batiks ceased. The process became once more the province of individual craftsmen in the Far East, while in Europe it was developed by artist craftsmen. Museums in Haarlem were, as a result of Holland's colonization in the east, a rich source of material, and it is therefore not surprising that a school of batik design, known as the Haarlem School, developed here. By 1900 batik had become a standard feature of arts and crafts exhibitions. The fine, decorative ornamentation gained influence in Holland, integrating Javanese and Dutch traditions and contributing to the art nouveau style. Among those whose names are associated with this development are Lebeau, Cachet, Prikker, Dijsselhof, Colenbrander, Bake and Pangon.

The most interesting application employed by

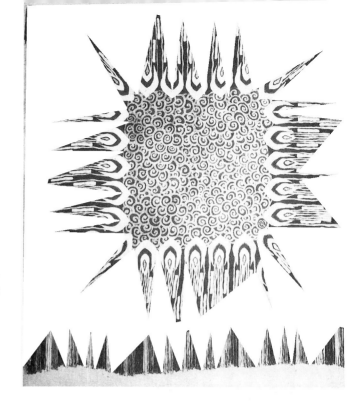

6 Lampshade by Madame Pangon
One of the few early women batik artists and, a member of the Haarlem School in 1905. Her first exhibition was in Marseilles in 1910. Later she moved to Paris, setting up a small batik factory in 1916 employing 50 people. She made many designs for clothes, shawls and interior fabrics and was very influential during the twenties, and can be traced in the work of Erté, Bakst and Diaghilev.

members of the Haarlem School was in the area of furniture production, where batik inlay was used to great effect. One member, Madame Pangon, moved to Paris, where she established a small factory in the Rue de la Boetie in 1916.

These far-reaching consequences of exposure to the batik art of the east can be seen in the work of many twentieth-century designers, among them Roger Fry and Charles Rennie Mackintosh.

AFRICA

A tradition of resist dyeing is also part of the history of Africa. For centuries the Yorubas of

Southern Nigeria and the Soninke and Wolof tribes of Senegal have practised crafts involving the use of resist. In the case of the Yorubas, cassava paste is used as the resist material, whilst the Soninke use rice paste. In recent times paraffin and stearin products have replaced the traditional materials in some areas. The mud cloths of the Bambara people of Mali are produced by a technique very closely aligned to that of batik. The cloths are dipped for a day in a dye produced by boiling the bark of certain trees. Mud from ferrous ponds is then applied with a scoop to produce a pattern and when this has dried the patterned areas are covered with a highly concentrated alkali soap produced by the Bambara people. The entire fabric is then covered with mud and dried in the sun; when the mud turns to dust it is removed and the fabric is rinsed. Where the alkali has bleached the cloth the pattern is revealed in a lighter colour on the dark background.

7 Adire Eleko
This design from Abeokuta, Nigeria, is produced by applying cassava paste resist through a stencil. The cloth is then dried and indigo dyed. The process is repeated over several days, dipping, airing and re-dipping and airing, to achieve the deep blue background. The paste is then scraped off to reveal the white design.

Motifs may be linked to traditional symbols as illustrated here, or may be produced to celebrate certain popular events.

CHINA, LAOS, VIETNAM AND THAILAND

It is certain that wax was used as a resist extensively in China, but today it is confined to the nomadic tribes who live on either side of the South China border. Foremost among these tribes are the Miao, who make batik clothes and are renowned for their unique costumes combining batik with appliqué and embroidery. The Miao originated from Kwei-Chow, but in the eighteenth century they emigrated to the Upper Tangking and the islands of Hainan. They applied their precise wax designs using a metal pen with a reservoir between two parallel sides of a triangular-shaped nib.

8 A woman from the Miao tribe drawing wax on a cloth. The molten beeswax is drawn on the cloth in geometrical patterns. The reservoir for the wax is contained between a folded triangular metal pen attached to a long handle.
(Photograph by Fu Muran)

Women work the cloth on a smooth board, heating wax from an iron pot and drawing the pen geometrically with only the cloth folds as a guide. The cloth is fairly coarse and in dyeing indigo the colour breaks through the wax resist in part to shade it blue.

9 Katazome – paste printing. *Japanese stencil cutters use steel-blade knives to cut finely organized patterns in laminated hand-made paper. The cloth is pasted down on a board, the stencil is laid on top and the paste is spread with a squeegee or hara.*

10 Katazome – filling in colour. *Colour is brushed within the stencilled paste outlines. Shading and edge colours are matched in with a variety of fine, specially-shaped brushes.*

INDIA
The main centres of batik today are on the south eastern part of the Deccan plateaux and the Coromande coast. The batik industry was at its peak in the seventeenth and eighteenth centuries when exports were made to many countries including Java, Persia and Europe. The trad-

11 Tsutsugaki – applying paste through a cone. *Before brushing the background colour on, the painted flower design has to be reserved. The glutinous rice paste is squeezed on and dried to resist the final colour. The paste is then washed, brushed and rinsed out of the cloth.*

*12 A kimono made using the bingata technique.
This is made of cotton, decorated with pines and
swallows, stencilled rice paste resist-dyed. It was
made in Okinawa in the nineteenth century.*
(Victoria & Albert Museum)

itional method used in the south eastern Deccan was batik combined with colouring and painting. The pen used for waxing is called a *kalam*. It consists of three parts: a metal needle set into a bamboo handle, wrapped in about 6cm of absorbent fibre or hair, which acts as a reservoir for the molten wax. Pressure on the wad regulates the flow.

The work of waxing is done by men, who must belong to the caste of indigo dyers. After the first waxing they prepare the cloth again for a further waxing and painting on of colour by a process of washing, beating and tanning. This latter process is considered comparatively easy and is usually completed by children.

JAPAN

During the eighth century AD batik, known in Japan as *roketsu-zome*, was a common way of

13 Manchester batiks made using machine roller print. The wax resin is printed on to the cloth, vat-dyed and then washed to remove some of the wax. The effect on re-dyeing gives the pattern a random, hand-produced effect.

dyeing cloth, having been introduced into the country by the Chinese. Apart from liquid wax being painted on as a resist, it was also applied with fine wooden stencils. This latter method was commonly used on the silk garments of warriors. Subsequent developments of an alternative resist led to a greater refinement of design and increased the popularity of batik. This method was known as *katazome*. It used a paste made of rice flour and bran that was applied through a cut-out paper stencil on to the cloth. Colour was brushed within the resist barriers, and then the water-soluble paste was washed

14 Batik Easter eggs. Pyssanka, predating Christ, originated in the Ukraine. Patterns are applied by using a funnel-shaped pen filled with molten beeswax. The method illustrated corresponds to the traditional over-dyeing and waxing except that the final removal of wax is done by warming the surface and rubbing the wax off with a cloth.

and cleaned off. An alternative method of application was by using a paper cone to draw the paste outlines – *Tjsutsugaki*. This more refined version, with the addition of delicate hand-painted pigments, produced the very distinguished *yuzen* style.

During the Edo period (1600–1868), Japan enjoyed a period of stability and could develop its cultural independence to the exclusion of any outside influence. The essence of the decorative richness of this time was reflected in the *kimono*, and an essential and explicit style developed which displayed the taste, profession or occasion more directly than has ever been possible on any garment in the west.

Since the 1920s *roketsu-zome* has regained popularity and is often integrated with other techniques of dyeing.

MACHINE WAX PRINTING

Since the mid-nineteenth century, the Dutch have been producing an industrial wax print, imitative of the Javanese style, for the African market. By the end of the century Britain, through its colonial development, opened up further markets which the Dutch could not cater for. The African print industry was begun in Manchester by Brunnschweiler, a division of

Tootal. In recent years through Africanization, native styles and designs have been demanded to replace European dress. In Nigeria alone, which has a population of over eighty-five million, a high preference was shown for the wax-print over other printed techniques. Today in Africa works have been set up to produce wax prints and in time will rival the quality of the imports and become independent. Many have now acquired the technical skills to reproduce their own distinctive designs. With the eventual self-sufficiency of the African countries in printing, interesting opportunities could arise for countries such as Britain, Holland and Japan to concentrate on designing and producing for home markets.

Technically, the African 'wax print' is a misnomer. The resist is in fact a resin. It is a natural dark brown and tacky in consistency when heated. The resist patterns are printed on the cloth by two engraved copper rollers rotating together. The resin is cooled and pulled through a pot-eye to remove and marble the resin before dyeing. The cloth is passed through an indigo vat; it then oxidizes and passes over a series of creepers or racks. This combined process of dipping and oxidizing is repeated four times to get the full depth of the indigo. Other colours are added after the cloth is washed and dried and treated with naphthol; the cloth is then passed through a bath of azodye, whereupon coupling takes place, and the colour develops.

Finally, the cloth is cleaned of resin, washed and finished.

two

TRADITIONAL BATIK TECHNIQUES

MATERIALS

Cotton is the most common material used in the making of batik garments in Java. Cotton cloths were worn by the people of Java and northern Sumatra as far back as the sixth and seventh centuries. There is evidence that during the Sung dynasty (960–1279) cotton goods from Java were customarily offered as princely gifts. In the fifteenth century they were exported to islands west of Borneo. At one time fine cotton cloth was imported from India, but since 1815 this has been supplanted by European imports. Today Java is also producing cambric in four grades – the finest primissima, prima, biru, and the coarsest merah.

The cotton is cut to the required length and has then to be freed of size. It is thoroughly boiled and washed, soaked in a bath and kneaded well by hand or under foot, after which it is dried out of doors. The process that follows this is known as mordanting, where the cloth is soaked in a mixture of oil and lye. Lye is obtained from the ashes of rice straw or the trunks of various types of banana plant. It is customarily mixed with castor oil or groundnut oil, or, more rarely, with sesame oil. If the cloth is to be dyed red with morinda the process of mordanting may last as long as 40 days. If, however, the material is to be dyed indigo or brown, the cloth is boiled only in a diluted solution of rice paste, to which a little lime and bamboo leaves are added.

The cloth is sized to prevent the liquid wax from penetrating into the fibres too freely. The size used is usually a diluted paste rice starch or cassava, sometimes with the addition of alum. The final process involves pounding the fabric with a wooden mallet. The resulting surface, rendered smooth and maleable, proves receptive to the drawing process which is the next stage in the production of batik.

Silk fabrics are mordanted in a bath of oil and lye for approximately two weeks but are not generally pre-washed. They are then spread on mats to dry, unlike cotton cloths, which are hung up on bamboo racks. They are subsequently sized. Silk is mostly reserved for the manufacture of *slendangs*.

The waxing process, which is traditionally done by women, follows. The cloths are hung over wooden or bamboo frames, and the main divisions are outlined in charcoal or pencil. The experienced batik worker may now proceed to draw the traditional patterns from memory or copy them from a finished cloth hung beside her as a model. In some cases she may employ a parchment stencil or pattern called *polas*, which she places beneath the fabric.

The instrument for the application of the wax is the *canting*. This consists of a small copper cup with one or more capillary spouts and a handle of reed or bamboo. The number of these spouts and their openings vary. For drawing outlines a canting with a very slender spout is used with which it is possible to draw a stroke about a millimetre ($\frac{1}{32}$in.) wide. For drawing ornaments consisting of a number of dots or lines at even distances, cantings with two to five or seven spouts are used. To cover small spaces a cup with

15 *Using the canting.*

a broad spout is used, while large spaces are filled with a crude brush formed by fastening a wad of cloth to the mouth of a canting.

The wax traditionally used is beeswax, customarily obtained from Timor, Sumbawa or Sumatra. In 1860, however, it began to be replaced by a cheaper European ozokerite from Galicia in eastern Europe, but since 1905 paraffin produced locally has replaced the ozokerite. Mixtures of beeswax, paraffin, microcrystalline resin and animal fat are common today, and the recipes are often closely-guarded secrets.

Heated in a pan of copper, iron or earthenware, the wax is maintained in a liquid state, at as even a temperature as possible, over an open fire. This is done on a small brick stove of cylindrical form called an *anglo* with a square opening on one side and sometimes a removable lid on top. When the melted wax has been carefully brought to the correct temperature, the worker fills the canting. Care is taken not to touch the cloth with the canting while drawing, and great skill is required in handling the instrument.

When one side of the material is waxed it is turned and hung over the rack against the sun to be reserved on the reverse side. This reserving process is done with various mixtures of wax – light and dark – so that the different sections of the design are clearly defined. Mixed waxes are strained through a cloth to prevent residue obstructing the smooth flow of the wax. Light wax is reserved for outlines and intricate designs, while large spaces are done with cheaper mixtures. It may take a worker between 30 and 50 days to make a sarong 2m (2yd) in length, depending on the complexity of the design.

The most difficult work is divided amongst experienced batik workers, who concentrate on the production of intricate detail, while novices are employed on reserving.

Veining is not a common element in traditional batiks as it was considered an imperfection. In indigo dyeing, the cloth is exposed to the sun long enough to keep the wax supple.

Rice-flour paste replaces beeswax as a resist material in more isolated districts in south-west Java. Cloths thus dyed are traditionally monochrome – turkey-red (*mengkudu*) – and the quality of such batiks tends to be crude. Cotton cloth is mordanted for 40 days by being repeatedly boiled in oil and lye and then washed and dried. It is then spread out horizontally between four pegs or laid flat on the ground. The surface is divided by small wooden sticks and the design drawn on with the rice paste. Occasionally, the designs are drawn with the fingers directly, with bamboo spoons or with a rag wrapped round a bamboo pin. For more intricate details bamboo quills are used. The dye, a cold turkey-red solution, is applied to the fabric with a broad brush. When the dyeing is completed, the paste is removed by soaking the whole cloth in cold water.

DYES AND DYEING METHODS

Natural indigo is the oldest dye traditionally used in Indonesia. It is also the only purely vat dye. Its importance in the dyeing of fabrics also extends to Asia and Africa, and where batik has not developed beyond a primitive stage, indigo is invariably the only dye-stuff employed.

The manufacture of indigo dyestuffs and the actual process of dyeing with indigo is also done by men. They add a coconut shell of natural indigo to a mixture of lime, sugar and water in a large container at midday. The mixture is stirred and left until the following morning when it is ready for use. If indigo white is required, sugar is added to transform the insoluble indigo blue into indigo white, which is soluble. The transformation comes about through a process of fermentation. To provide the necessary alkali content lime is added.

Dyeing starts in the early morning and is carried out in wide, glazed receptacles. The cloths are steeped for two to three hours, dried in the air and then steeped again. During this process it is imperative that the cloths are completely covered by the liquid dye or small spots may appear. The dyeing process lasts for six to ten days, depending on the strength of colour required. Occasionally the process may take even longer, though methods of shortening it have been devised. If, for example, the fabric is treated with a solution of finely pounded bark of *Rhizophoracea ceriops candolleana arn* after each dipping, the process may be further accelerated. If synthetic indigo is used with an addition of ferrous sulphate and lime, the process may be shortened to two days. If a black colour is desired repeated dyeings with indigo will achieve the required result. An alternative method is to cover a dark indigo with brown.

Women traditionally carry out the red and brown dyeing. The dyestuff used for red is a mixture of dyer's morinda (root bark of *Morinda citrifolia* L.) and the bark of *Symplocos fasciculata zoll*, in the proportion of one-to-one or two-to-one. The fabric, which has previously been mordanted in oil and ash lye, is placed in a flat receptacle, and the dye is poured over it. The dye is rubbed in by hand, and, this process is repeated for 24 days.

The dyestuff for browns is more variable. Usually it consists of the bark of the soga tree, the tingi tree, 'yellow wood', or tegerang. Varnishing resin, colophonium and sugar are added to these in the Yogykarta area, but gambir and sugar are added in Semarang. Repeated steaming and additions of water disolve the ingredients. Dyeing in the case of browns takes place in lukewarm water, unlike blue and red dyeing, which is always cold. The temperature must not exceed 112°F (45°C) as this would melt the layer of wax. This process lasts between one and eight days. Brown colours have to be fixed. This is generally done in plain lime water, but for finer work special substances are used. These determine the different shades of brown and are generally well-guarded secrets. In the main, they contain various proportions of saltpetre, alum, quicklime, borax, lemon juice and crystalline sugar.

In the past it was possible to identify the batiks of different regions by their distinctive colours. For example, the batiks of Yogyakarta were distinguished by their clear, bright whites; those of Surakarta by being a softer cream. Both regions are traditionally limited to dark blue and brown colours. The batiks of Indramayu were noted for combinations of blue and black and those of Pekalongan for their vivid and varied colours, while Cirebon batiks were famous for the use of landscapes on a rich ivory background. Now, however, the use of synthetic indigo, alizarin for red, auramines and aniline has wiped out the distinctions brought about by local variations in dye-stuffs and procedures.

Before synthetic dyes, the natural colourants were indigo, turkey red from morinda and yellow from curcuma and cudriana. Greens were obtained by over-dyeing light blue with yellow, and black, as already explained, by repeated dyeings with indigo or over-dyeing dark indigo with brown. The predominance of delicate and subdued shades in traditional batiks was, to a large extent, the consequence of a restricted number of dye-stuffs from natural sources and their tendency to fade rapidly when exposed to tropical sunlight.

Today, as a result of the introduction of artificial colourants, this subtlety of colouring is no longer the main characteristic of the batik art of Indonesia, though the old cloths are still treasured and sought after.

Monochrome batiks

Cloths with monochrome blue or red patterns are the simplest known form of batik. These are the result of using a thin, very warm resist. Where dye-stuffs are applied to a lightly-sized fabric the colour penetrates to the other side. The pattern does not appear as distinctly on the reverse side of the cloth. Either the background is dyed and the pattern reserved or the design is dyed and the resist applied to the background – a process which requires more time and material. Cloths with white, undyed backgrounds are considered to be of better quality.

Small dots on a light background are a popular pattern found mainly on sarongs and sashes of silk or fine cotton with a simple blue design. This pattern is obtained by puncturing the wax with needles to allow the dye to penetrate as far as the cloth. A block-like instrument containing ten to forty needles is used for this process.

Polychrome batiks

In making polychrome batiks, indigo is usually applied first. (The island of Madura is distinctive in not observing this rule.) If a batik is to be red and brown or red and blue, red is the first colour to be applied. When the blue-dyed cloth has been thoroughly rinsed and dried, the wax resist is removed by being melted off in boiling water or by being scratched off with an implement or by hand.

After each dyeing process, the fabric must be sized again with rice-starch paste. The material is thoroughly washed and dried and freed from any trace of resist in a bath of boiling water.

SOGA KEROKAN

The principles of batik are the same, but the step-by-step procedures vary according to the region. In central Java the best known method is called *soga kerokan*. The following steps show the principle most clearly.

(1) The cloth is first cut into the traditional length for a batik: *kain* 2.5 × 1.05m (2yd 2′ × 1yd 4″), which is then hemmed to prevent fraying.

(2) Manufactured cloth is usually full of dressing and therefore it has to be washed and rinsed and washed again until clear.

(3) Starch made of rice or cassava is applied so that the wax will adhere more readily to a smooth and firm surface. In addition, the cloth is oiled for extra fine work, to facilitate more wax control.

(4) The cloth is beaten with a mallet to make it more supple.

(5) Once the motifs are learnt, the batik worker draws the wax on from memory.

(6) Two types of wax are applied to the cloth in the first waxing: *klowong* wax is light and brittle and will be easily removed after the first dyeing; *tembok* wax is stronger and will remain on the finished cloth to reserve the white areas of the design. Because the cloth will be dyed repeatedly the wax must be extremely resistant and flexible and would be considered inferior work if it broke down or marbled.

(7) The reverse of the cloth is also waxed exactly to the design to ensure that the colour is completely protected and clear in the finished cloth.

(8) Dyeing with indigo is a tradition that is passed from father to son. The making of the dye has all kinds of superstitions attached to it, and the process is a sacred ritual. The cloth is dipped between 20 and 60 times, suspended from a rack that usually holds about 20 waxed batiks at one time. The item is exposed for 15 minutes to oxidize before redipping. It is a very long and complex procedure and takes many days before the right depth of colour appears. After repeated use, the dye becomes weak and needs revitalizing by the addition of indigo-paste, iron vitriol and lime.

(9) After dyeing the brittle *klowong* wax is removed by the batiker first soaking the cloth in cold water to harden the wax. A scraper made of tin or a knife takes the wax off both surfaces. The white parts of the design are now exposed for the next dyeing, whilst the stickier wax remains to protect the white pattern throughout the successive dips.

(10) The cloth is rinsed in cold water to remove any *klowong* wax on its surface. A little soda is added to free any residue.

(11) Before the final dyeing in soga, a second waxing is applied to the indigo blue areas

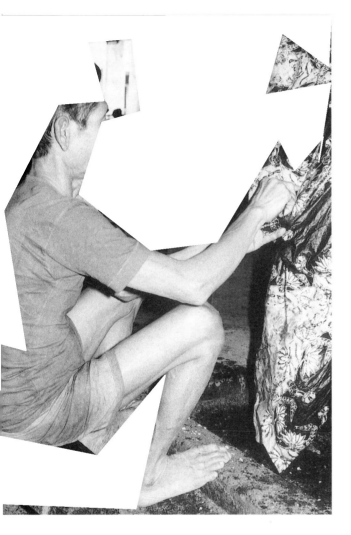

16 Scraping off wax. After the initial waxing and dyeing, part of the wax design is carefully scraped off to be dyed soga brown whilst the remaining wax will continue to protect the white areas during subsequent dyeings.

for economy as it has to survive only for the final dyeing.

Besides the indigo blue being covered with wax to compound the design, repairs are made to the *tembok* wax. If any breaks have occurred during handling, a heated nail is applied to fuse the wax together.

(12) The cloth is washed carefully and finally dyed in the brown known as soga.

(13) The soga vat is smaller than the indigo, vat, and each piece is dipped by hand. The pieces are dipped between 15 and 30 times and finally fixed.

(14) The finished wax and dyed cloth is then placed in a cauldron of boiling water containing soda ash or caustic soda to remove the wax. After the cloth has been agitated with a stick the wax floats to the surface and is scooped off and recycled.

(15) Once the wax is removed, the cloth is then finished by being washed thoroughly in a soapy solution.

PEKALONGAN METHOD

Since the introduction of synthetic dyes, an old technique has been revived for producing multicoloured contemporary batik. Originally, the painted-on technique was introduced from India, but was replaced by the rewaxing and overdyeing processes to produce many coloured combinations. The method, called *coletan*, does not require the cloth to be dipped for each colour. As the wax does not have to be removed after each dyeing, the process is much quicker and more predictable. Outlines of wax are drawn around motifs, and indigosol dyes are

to protect the colour. Where the brown overdyes the exposed blue it will create black. For this waxing a third kind of composition is used called *biron* which need not have the flexibility or brittle quality of the previous waxings. It is usually made of scraps of boiled-off wax

17 Pekalongan batik – detail of a 1930s sarong. The Chinese influence on batik was considerable especially on the north coast of Java. Oey Soe Tjoen, whose work is illustrated here, made some of the finest batiks, unusual for their use of the European irises in this design.
(Rudolf Smend Collection)

18 Making a cap.

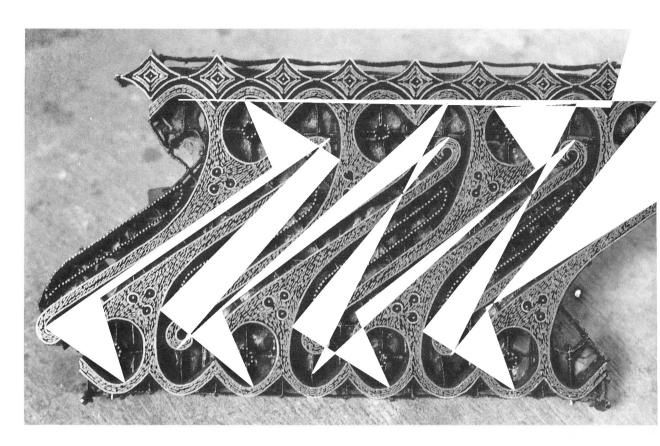

brushed directly into them; the wax prevents bleeding of the colour. These motifs are then sealed, and the background colour dipped or, alternatively, left the ground colour of the cloth.

Procedure

(1) Prepare cloth and pencil in design.
(2) Wax outlines of motif and cover areas which will eventually be dyed brown.
(3) Select and brush in colours within wax borders.
(4) Wax coloured areas.
(5) Immerse cloth in indigo, or intended background colour.
(6) Remove wax by boiling in water.
(7) Wax all areas except those to be dyed brown.
(8) Immerse cloth in soga brown.
(9) Finally remove wax in boiling water.

19 Cap block. This is made by soldering fine copper strips and pins into a pattern. Small pins, which align one wax impression with the next, are attached to the corners. A cloth design may employ many interlocking blocks. Another block common to the north coast is made up of sharp pins that puncture the solid wax areas to allow the dye to penetrate, enlivening a pale background with dark spots.

CAP PRINTING

Most Javanese batiks are stamp-printed today for economy. In the mid-nineteenth century the cap revolutionized the production of batiks and turned it into a thriving industry.

The making of the cap is an individual craft: it involves cutting out the patterns from rolls of sheet copper and attaching them to a frame so that they form a level impression when applied to the cloth.

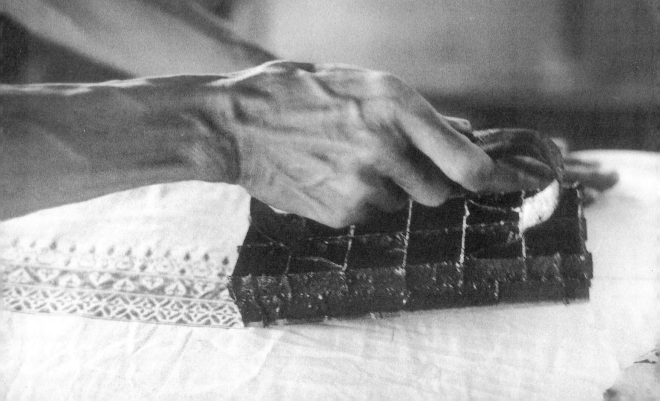

20 *Wax pan. Melted wax for stamping is heated in a pan containing an absorbent pad, which acts as a filter to ensure that any impurities do not get transferred to the cloth.*

21/22 *Cap printing. A copper block to apply wax to a cloth speeds up the process; this revolutionized the batik industry in 1840. The cloth is spread on a padded table, the cap dipped into the wax and the design imprinted on the cloth. Tulis is sometimes combined as a refinement.*

The repetitive quality of the stamp designs can be distinguished from the hand-drawn ones. However, to the layman the difference is not easy to define, particularly if the patterns are made up of many small interrelated stamps. Sometimes as many as 16 are used and usually pairs of stamps are made for printing on both sides of the cloth. Mirror image fitting is essential for registration and clarity and different compositions of wax resist require separate blocks as well.

The cap printing is carried out on an angled table, padded and kept moist by applying a

diluted lye solution. This ensures that the wax doesn't stick to the table when the stamp is applied. The wax is heated in a pan containing a porous cushion, which soaks up any impurities in the wax that may spoil the printing. The cap printer dips the stamp into the wax pan then lifts and taps off any excess wax that may clog the pattern. The temperature has to be judged correct before the stamp is applied to the cloth, edge-on first for registration. Full pressure is then applied and the stamp released when the impression has been made. After completing one side, the cloth is reversed and the matching wax stamps are applied to confirm a complete resist.

According to custom, this work is done by men.

TRADITIONAL PATTERNS

The greatest variety of batik patterns employed stem from Java. There are at least a thousand patterns which can be exactly defined and bear names such as moonshine charm, boar at night and waddling goose. These patterns are an amalgamation of ornamentations drawn from a wide variety of periods and places, including India, China, Japan and, in the case of more modern batiks, Europe. The patterns can be classified within four basic types:

The semen

This pattern usually reveals a non-Javanese influence in natural shapes such as leaves and flowers combined with the *lar* or wing motif, which is found either in pairs or singly, and the mountain and cloud motif, believed to be Chinese in origin.

The ceplok

This is a continuous symmetrical pattern of natural units seen from above and formed into circles and squares based on a microscopic

23 Javanese dancers rehearsing. They are wearing the classic parang *motif on their* kains.

observation of natural forms. These stars, rosettes and crosses are generally arranged in symmetrical groups such as the *ganggong*. The names of such patterns, despite their formalized appearance, point to their origin in natural forms.

Another form of ceplokken design is based on the patterns formed by plaited or woven fabrics or fibres. The effect here is achieved by a series of dots and dashes placed at regular intervals.

The parang

This slanting diagonal-stripe pattern contains smaller geometrical floral repeat patterns. These motifs were generally reserved for the garments of princes, nobles and court officials. This ornamental border originated in China and is most commonly to be found in the form of a meander, forming borders or backgrounds. The purpose of the symbol was to avert evil.

The kawung

This motif is composed of a series of ellipses or ovals arranged in groups of four. This is a very ancient pattern derived from Persia and connected with forbidden ornaments.

Perhaps the oldest known Indonesian design is the *gringsing* or fish-scale pattern usually employed as a background. True to the dictates of Islam the human figure does not appear, with the exception of those occasions when figures from the *wayang* plays are used, and here the fish-scale pattern customarily appears as the background.

A strange horned animal with scales occurs in the batik work of northern Java and is thought to be Chinese in origin, while the phoenix and the fish – a Chinese symbol of fertility – appear in Cirebon batiks.

In more recent times in northern Java, batiks depicting scenes of native life have appeared. Again, these could be ascribed to Chinese influences.

In most other parts of the world the patterns are less varied than in Indonesia. Many of them are confined to the use of indigo and white and

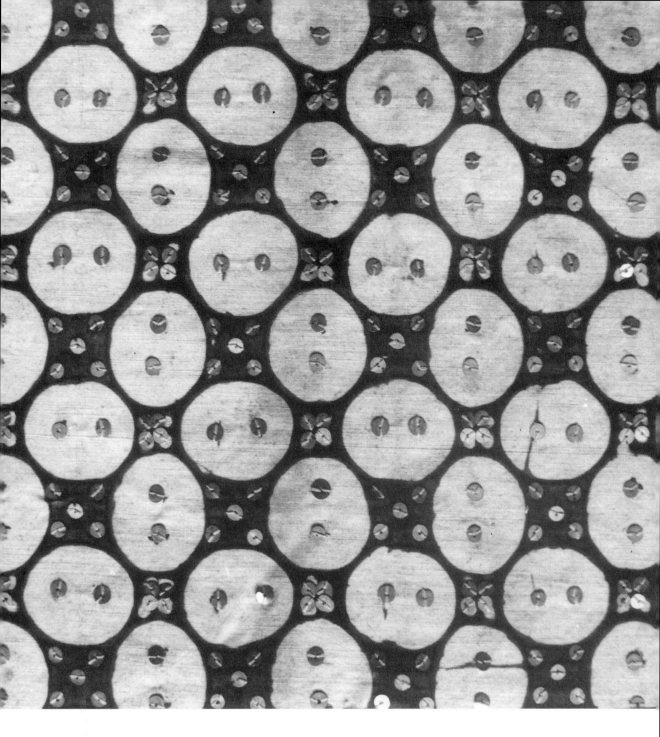

24 Pekalongan 1930–40 – detail of pants for men. The pattern is alternating flower bouquets and birds in tree branches. The border is an imitation fringe of floral vine and cloud motifs. (Rudolf Smend Collection)

25 Kawung pattern. This motif may have evolved from fish scales. It is a very ancient design, reflecting the belief in a universal structure. The cross represents its source of energy. The colours used are soga brown, black and cream. It was made in Central Java. (Rudolf Smend Collection)

most are geometric and far simpler in design than Indonesian motifs.

TRADITIONAL GARMENTS

To some extent ornamentation in batik is dictated by the type of garment for which it is designed.

The iket kepala

A large headcloth about 1m (3ft) square, this is worn only by men. It is customarily decorated with motifs distributed over its entire surface, but at the centre there is a plain diamond shape which is left undyed in contrast to the patterned frame, although, on occasions, it is dyed plain indigo, red or yellow. This diamond is sometimes framed by a frieze of *cemukirans*, or small pointed leaves, which alter from district to district. Occasionally, too, the border of the garment imitates a fringe.

The kemben and the slendang

These are long shawl-like cloths of about 50–250cm ($\frac{1}{2}$–$2\frac{1}{2}$yd) in size. Javanese dancers wear sashes which are slightly narrower. The *kimben* is a breast cover which is rarely worn today, but the more traditional *slendang* is slung over one shoulder and is often used to carry babies or provisions. Traditionally, these cloths are covered entirely with patterns though they may also have an unpatterned rectangle in the centre. If this pattern takes the form of an elongated lozenge the cloth is known as *blumbangan* and has staight or scalloped sides. Alternatively, if it is a rectangle the same shape as the cloth it is called *sundangen*. These cloths are decorated with borders and the central lozenge or rectangle is defined by cemukiran motifs.

The sarong

This is a waist-cloth, used by both men and women. It is on this garment that the traditional arrangement of the ornaments is most significant. The sarong covers the body and legs from the waist down to the ankles and may be made of cotton or silk fabric. It is about 107 × 180cm ($3\frac{1}{2}$ × 6ft) in length. It is either wrapped around the hips and thus secured, or sewn into the shape of an open sack into which the wearer steps. This garment is drawn tight on one side and fastened upon itself in a knot or secured with a belt.

The ornamentation of the sarong is divided into three parts: the centre piece called the *kepala*, flanked by two large wings. The *kepala* carries a strictly geometric design which remains the same on all sarongs and the two wings are more elaborately decorated. The *kepala* contains two rows of narrow triangles with points facing one another and is framed on each side by narrow borders called *papam* or *cumpak*. The top and bottom seams of the sarong are bordered by a very narrow ornamented stripe. The designs on the side parts vary from district to district. Sarongs may have different patterns at each end and are called *pagi-sore* meaning morning-evening. By folding the cloth different ways their use is altered.

The kain

This is a longer, more formal cloth than the sarong used by both men and women. The entire cloth is decorated with borders at the short ends; it is wrapped around the waist with the last 50cm (20in.) arranged as pleats at the back of the body.

The dodot

This is larger than the sarong and may be twice as long. With a plain lozenge-shaped centre surrounded by even patterning, *dodots* are worn with a train or a large hanging fold on the side. This is a formal garment, worn by princes, court dancers, high officials and wedding couples.

26 Kepala. The design of a sarong usually features a 'head' which contrasts with the main pattern. The most common is a tumpal, a spear-like motif which is worn in the front by women and at the back by men. Red, blue, black and cream colours are used – and gold for celebrations. (Rudolf Smend Collection)

l of a sarong made on the north coast of
1920. It depicts a battle scene between
se and Dutch soldiers. In hand-drawing the
had license to design and explore current
ts.
.dolf Smend Collection)

**28 Arjuna and Sumbadra in audience with Prabu
Parameswara by K. Kuswadji**
Kuswadji pioneered the use of batik as a painting
medium in Indonesia. His style, depicting classical
legends, quickly became famous through his
numerous exhibitions in Europe. He also
contributed to the setting up of the Batik Research
Centre in 1969. The state honoured his
achievements by providing a studio and gallery
close to the Palace in Jogykarta where both his
and his son's work, can be viewed.

29 *Applying fluid resist to cloth and dyeing is
radically different from creating a printed, imposed
image. Dyeing integrates with the cloth to create a
new definition of the 'art-fabric'. Batik calls for
technical skills and a study of the Indonesian
techniques, but also unadorned intuition and
creativity. Choice and change are its essence.*

three

MODERN BATIK

The contemporary batik artist setting up a workshop has access to excellent materials and, since the requirements are few, he or she should acquire and employ only the very best. There is no advantage in resorting to experimental use of poor quality tools and fabric – the result is likely to be frustrating and disappointingly amateurish.

Abundant supplies and choice of refined fabrics, dyes, waxes, cantings and brushes on the market leave no excuse for this approach to the art of batik. With perserverance and the development of manual skills and the aid of an imaginative approach to the craft, the artist can enjoy the unique value that this medium offers for self expression.

THE WORKSHOP

The first requirement in setting up a workshop is, of course, space. Where a workshop is, by necessity, small, take great care to plan the area so that it yields the maximum efficiency in production and safety.

- Natural light is a prime requirement as it makes the judgement of colour so much more possible; in its absence, good, even, electric lighting is essential.
- Ventilation must also be given careful con-

sideration as wax fumes can cause irritation. An efficient electric extractor fan is the best solution.

- The working surfaces themselves must be smooth, stable and durable. Put plastic sheeting on the floor to provide a protective surface.
- The workshop should, if possible, have a liberal supply of electric points or overhead leads of the track variety for connecting to wax heaters, fans, etc.
- A large sink with a supply of hot and cold water is a necessity.
- Air-tight containers to store dyes away from heat and light are useful; they should be clearly labelled and dated.
- A supply of enamel bowls, heat-proof measuring jugs and measuring spoons is essential. For dip-dyeing, shallow plastic baths are recommended as they are inexpensive and easy to manipulate.
- To heat the wax a thermostatically-controlled container is the most practical. Alternatively, use a small stable saucepan and a hot-plate.
- Use a good quality measuring scale, preferably with a double scale (0–50g. and 0–500g.).
- A drying line area away from direct sunlight is also needed.

FABRICS

For the best results cloth made from natural fibres is recommended. The only man-made fibre that can be considered for use in the production of batiks is Viscose Rayon.

Cotton

Cotton, either wild or cultivated, has been in use as a textile fibre for several thousands of years. One fragment, known to be 3000 years old and of Indian origin, has survived and it is generally supposed that India was the birthplace of cotton fabric. However, Egypt is also the home of cotton, and some authorities claim that cotton was used in Egypt as early as 12,000 BC. Cotton was hand-woven in Spain by the tenth century AD though when Indian cotton was brought to Europe by travellers in the sixteenth and seventeenth centuries the superiority of the Indian product was widely recognized. In the Americas, cotton was indigenous to Peru, and cotton cloth was discovered in Mayan cities dating from 632 BC. Mexico has yielded fragments identified as being 7000 years old. In North America cotton was cultivated first in the state of Virginia in 1607 and with the invention by Eli Whitney of the cotton gin, a machine which facilitated the extraction of the seeds from the raw cotton, the cotton industry was established.

Cotton is a hair attached to the seed of several species of the genus *Gossypium*, a shrub that grows between 120 and 180cm (4 and 6ft) high indigenous to nearly all tropical regions; it flourishes near the sea, lakes or large rivers where there is a warm, humid climate and sandy soil. Today the main cotton-producing areas are Egypt, the southern United States of America, India, Brazil, the West Coast of Africa, the West Indies, the USSR and China. The best crops are obtained by cultivating the plants annually.

Cotton is an ideal fibre. Each fibre has 20 to 30 layers of cellulose built up in an orderly series of spring-like spirals. When the cotton ball opens the fibres dry into flat, twisted, ribbon-like shapes and become interlocked. This makes an ideal form for spinning into fine yarn. These characteristics of the fibre account for the durability, absorbency, wet-strength and softness of cotton. Because the fibre is hollow it can absorb a great deal of moisture. The outer layer of cellulose contains a wax which gives surface smoothness and a natural lustre to the fabric. It is, accordingly, an ideal material for subjecting to the action of dyes as the fibres can scarcely be damaged by their action.

An immense variety of cloths are manufactured from cotton: voile, organdie, lawn, satin, poplin, pique, corduroy, velvet, repp, denim, gaberdine and the cloth we call cotton.

Linen

In Egypt and the Near East linen as a cloth was established by 3000 BC. The earliest examples of printed linen known today date from the fifth century AD but records indicate that it existed from 2500 BC. A combination of linen and cotton known as *fustion* and consisting of a linen warp and a cotton weft was the earliest type of fabric used in textile printing in Europe.

Linen is woven from yarn made from the fibres of the flax plant, a member of the family *Linaceae*. The flax plant has blue or white flowers and grey-green stems and grows to a height of 95–120cm (3–4ft). The types grown for fibre branch only at the top of the stem. The flax plant grows best in temperate climates, free from heavy rains, but where moist winds occur during the growing season.

The best quality flax in use comes from Ireland, but flax cultivation ceased in Northern Ireland in 1954 and even before that, by 1950, it was no longer a commercial crop. Flax is still grown in Southern Ireland at Bunclody. Most of the fibre used in the linen industry in Ireland, however, is imported from France and the USSR. The Russian fibre is inferior in quality as it is short and strong.

Flax is not cut but is pulled from the ground when the green stems begin to turn yellow. Today this action is performed entirely by

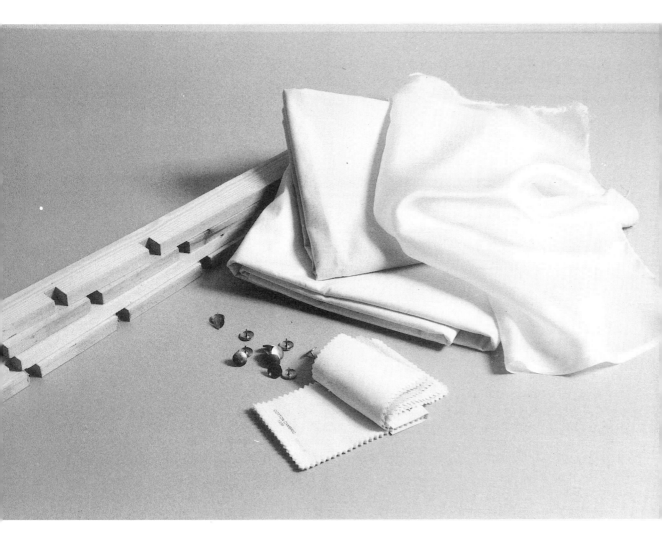

machines. Then comes the important process known as retting, which disposes of the woody part of the stems. Originally accomplished by soaking in water, this process is now virtually extinct and has been replaced by dew retting, which is carried out on the ground through the action of bacteria, moisture and light. At the spinning stage the use of chemicals ensures the even result dependent on fibre separation. After retting the flax is dried and then beaten, or scutched, to break the pith and free the fibres with as little damage as possible.

The best fibre is pale yellow in colour, flexible and lustrous, though by comparison with cotton yarn, linen is more irregular.

30 Fabrics
Fine cotton and silks are the best materials to work with; here they are shown with an adjustable frame to support the cloth.

Silk

The Chinese held a monopoly on silk production for about 3000 years, although it is possible that India produced silk as early as 1000 BC. The secret of sericulture was smuggled out of China by two Persian monks who disguised themselves as Christian missionaries and transported a small quantity of silkworm eggs out of China hidden in a hollow cane. The secrets they had

31 Within
Folded silk, 52 × 72cm, 1981.

gathered about silk production were given to the
Emperor Justinian, and in AD 552 he proclaimed
a monopoly on the trade. Arabs brought this
knowledge to Sicily and Italy, and for centuries
Lucca in northern Italy was the centre of the silk-
weaving industry. By the thirteenth century
Lyons and Tours in France were also established
silk-weaving areas.

The main source of contemporary silk is the
Chinese moth *Bombyx mori*. This is an ash-
coloured moth whose caterpillar feeds on mulberry leaves, converting the albumen content of
the leaves into liquid silk which it stores in
its body. Silk is extruded through two spinnerets
on either side of the head, and the cocoon is
thus formed. If the moth is allowed to emerge
from the cocoon in the normal way the threads
are damaged. Accordingly, the cocoons are
hot-air dried to kill the chrysalis within. The

Turn About. *Cotton, 120 x 95 cm, 1984.*

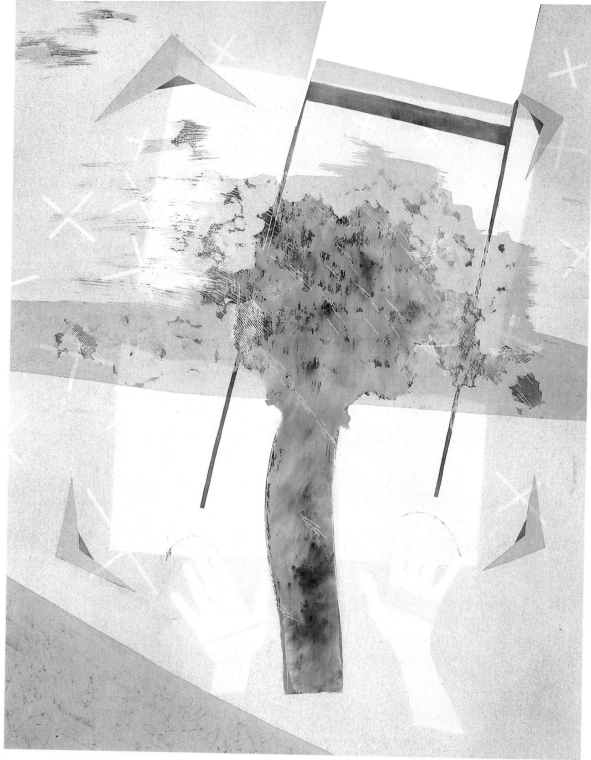

Bouquet. *Cotton, naphthol and reactive dyes,*
120 x 95 cm, 1983.

Javanese Dancer.

Applying wax with a canting.

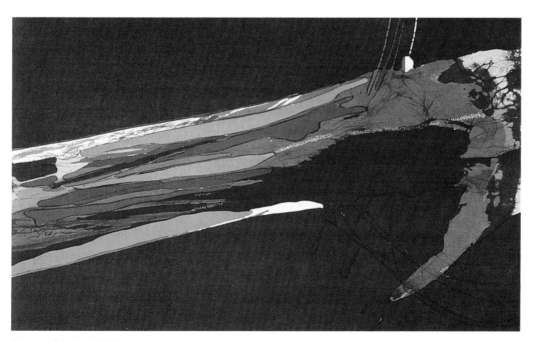

Swamp by Amri Yahya.
Cotton, naphthol and indigosol dyes, 1981.

Ariel. *Cotton, stencil spray, naphthol and reactive dyes, 120 x 95 cm, 1983.*

Pan. *Veneer, 120 x 180 cm, 1986.*

Winter Sky. *Cotton, 120 x 95 cm, 1981.* (Private collection).

Tropic Slice. *Cotton, discharge and reactive dyes, 120 x 95 cm, 1987.*

outer part of the cocoon is then discarded and the middle section boiled to soften the gum which seals it. The end of the thread is then located and the silk wound onto a frame. The average silkworm yields about 1800m (2000yd) of thread, but only about 457m (500yd) are used as continuous filament. The other silk-producing moths, found mostly in Asia, live on oak and other leaves and produce tussah, shantung and honan, which are all wild silks.

Natural silk is one of the strongest textile fibres, having a stretched-out molecular form. Once de-gummed, it has a tensile strength of 4–5 grams per denier. By contrast softened steel has a rate of 3 grams. Silk fibres can be extended to 20–25 per cent of their length before breaking. Silk is available in a wide variety of textures and weights; the smooth type is best for batik.

Wool

Wool has been spun and woven by man from as early as the seventh century BC. Wool and hair are fibres of protein which emerge from the hair follicles coated with grease.

Fleeces sheared during the warm season contain between only 43 and 50 per cent wool by weight. The remaining weight is composed of oils, fats, moisture and dirt. Wool fibre is enclosed in irregular everlapping scales with cell tissue inside them. The outer cuticle is resistant to wetting, but moisture in vapour form can be absorbed by the fibres.

There are hundreds of wool fabrics, but for batik the best are crêpes, jersey, lightweight plain weaves such as Liberty varuna and mixtures such as Viyella.

PREPARATION OF FABRICS

Today, most commercially available fabrics have already been scoured to remove foreign matter and bleached to be as white as possible. Before work can be carried out, however, it is advisable to test the fabric for dye-absorption and streaking. If there are indications that the fabric contains impurities it will then be necessary to pre-treat it before work starts on the batik process. In many cases, a good soak in warm water, followed by thorough rinsing, may be sufficient; alternatively, the fabric may be machine-washed. Rinse the fabric thoroughly before dry and iron damp.

In immersion-dyeing this scouring process is perhaps not quite so vital as the long period in the dye-bath ensures that the dye penetrates the fibres. In brush or spray-dyeing, however, when the period of absorption is necessarily far shorter, scrupulous scouring is essential.

If silk has to be treated it is necessary to excercise the greatest care. The silk should be soaked in water at a temperature of 158°F (70°C) for about 30 minutes. Three per cent soda ash may be added to the water and the addition of a little white vinegar to the final rinse should ensure that the fabric is freed of all impurities. A water-softener is also a good addition and renders the fabric more receptive to the dyes.

WAX

The quality of the resist depends primarily on the composition and diverse nature of the waxes available. *Beeswax*, traditionally used, is strong and durable but is not resistant to alkali and can cause unresolved breaks when dyed. *Microcrystalline wax*, a synthetic with similar properties, adheres and penetrates the fabric easily. *Paraffin wax* has a lower melting point, is thin and tends to crack or flake off the material. Resins are hard and sticky but also marble very easily. They are difficult to dissolve and can congeal. Fat has a very low melting point, is greasy and contributes a greater flexibility to a recipe. You can vary the formulas and experiment by adding a little of this to that; soon you

32 Waxes. Specially prepared wax is available, but
for versatile effects you can mix your own using
paraffin, and microcrystalline together with
beeswax, resins and gums.

will be able to control these proportions to attain the desired outcome. Be careful, however: too much paraffin wax may cause the dye to undermine the imagery. Preparation of the recipes is crucial to the result.

A commercial 'ready-made' batik wax consists of paraffin and microcrystalline waxes in the ratio 2:1. This usually comes in a granulated form.

Here are some resist wax recipes to try:

a. **General purpose wax**
   1 part beeswax
   1 part microcrystalline wax
   1 part paraffin

b. **Strong wax suitable for canting**
   6 parts pine resin
   4 parts paraffin
   1 part beeswax
   0.25 parts damor gum
   0.25 parts fat

c. **Blocking wax for covering areas**
   2 parts beeswax
   1 part pine resin
   0.5 parts damor gum
   0.5 parts microcrystalline wax
   0.1 parts fat

d. **Crackle wax – brittle for marble effects**
   5 parts paraffin wax
   5 parts pine resin
   1 part damor gum
   0.2 parts fat

The subtlety and strength of the wax resistance to the compounding dyeing sequences can be controlled by the following:

- Composition and amount of different waxes
- Temperature – different levels of wax penetration into the cloth
- Style of application – brush, canting, block, spray etc.

Method
Add the ingredients one by one, from the highest melting point to the lowest.

Damor gum 176°F (80°C)
Pine resin 176°F (80°C)
Microcrystalline 167°F (75°C)
Beeswax 136°F (58°C)
Paraffin 122°F (50°C)
Fat 122°F (50°C)

Safety precautions

- Do not over-heat wax as it may ignite. Maintain a temperature of about 136°F (58°C).
- Should fire occur smother pot of wax with lid or douse with bicarbonate of soda.
- Keep away from an open flame.
  Clean hot-plate regularly of overspilt wax.

THE WAX POT
To melt the wax you need a substantial metal pan or pot, thermostatically-controlled, with a stable base. Make sure this does not over-heat or the wax will smoke. An electric frying pan is also very practical as it is low and shallow and can accommodate a number of individual cans of different waxes. The alternatives are an electrical hot plate with controls or a double boiler with a water compartment. The latter, whilst protecting the wax from direct heat has the disadvantage of not heating up the wax sufficiently.

33 Wax pots. Electrical, thermostatically controlled pots for melting the wax are more practical. These can be in the form of an electric frying pan or a purpose-built container. An electric cooking ring with a secure saucepan is an alternative.

34 Cantings. These range from electric cantings to different styles of tools from Malaysia, Sri Lanka and Japan. The finest are from Indonesia.

Maintaining a constant temperature of about 136°F (58°C) is important. By burning the 'fatty' content in the wax the elastic properties are reduced. Impurities in the wax can be filtered off through a muslin cloth.

TOOLS
There are a number of tools used for applying molten wax to cloth. The canting and brush are the traditional tools associated with batik, while block stamps and rollers with surfaces adapted for the retention of wax are associated with printing fabric. More random methods of applying wax such as splattering have now found their place in batik-making. Look after your tools and use them with imagination and flexibility.

Cantings
The canting is a small, spouted metal cup for applying wax. It comes in many sizes and may have up to seven spouts. The spouts used are for drawing parallel lines or dots, or, alternatively, for filling in solid areas. The canting is like a pen and may be employed to create the most intricate and refined designs; as such it is an indispensable tool. The cantings of Javanese origin have yet to be bettered.

Handling the canting is a matter of some skill but almost anyone can become adept at regulating the even outflow of wax by following a few rules and practising them regularly:

- Hold the canting in a relaxed position, saddled between the forefinger and the thumb.
- When filling the canting keep it in the molten wax until it is hot enough to allow the wax to flow consistently from the spout.
- Fill to only the half-way mark to avoid spilling wax over the work.
- Have a ready supply of absorbent material to wipe the spout and base of the cup before applying it to the cloth.
- When drawing, handle the canting so that you work horizontal to the fabric.

- Draw the tip of the spout slightly above the surface to release a smooth and consistent flow of wax. By pressing the canting on the cloth, the flow is blocked and penetration unreliable.
- Steady your hand by using the little finger as a stabilizer.
- Work from left to right when drawing a straight line. Complete a circle in two half movements to ensure consistency of line.
- When 'dotting', work rhythmically.
- Refuel before the wax is too cool to penetrate the cloth. You can judge this by the opaque quality of the the wax.
- If the flow of wax is impeded by impurities use a small piece of fuse wire to unblock the spout.
- If you wish to slow the flow of wax, cool it by blowing into the spout.

35 A relaxed hold on the canting.

36 Cleaning wax off the exterior.

37 Cleaning the spout

Brushes

For waxing

A range of brushes will give the batik-maker greater freedom and adaptability. Some brushes can be cut to different shapes. For filling in large patterned areas a broad brush of good quality natural hair or bristle is recommended. This will ensure that as much wax as possible is drawn up by the large brush to give greater coverage. Generally, a stiff brush is better than a soft one as it will force the wax more vigorously into the fabric. For finer work that can rival the quality of the canting line a round hair brush with a flexible point can be handled either with precision or an expressive fluency. A Chinese or Japanese *sumi*-style brush is ideal as it has a full head to act as a reservoir serving its fine point. Take care not to damage or distort the brushes, especially the finer, more fragile hair type.

Before you use new brushes place them in a

39 In the main, the brushes shown are used for painting on the dye and are made of fine but tightly packed natural fibre. For waxing, the brush should have a more substantial fibre content to sustain the effect of the molten wax. Well-worn brushes frequently give additional character to the work.

lower temperature wax to ensure an even penetration and protection. After this they can be cooled and shaped in preparation for use with higher temperature wax. Once brushes are in constant use do not leave them in the wax as they will rapidly burn and become mishapen and consequently difficult to use. Wax-impregnated brushes should never be left to harden against a work surface. Keep your brushes regularly pruned of burnt bristles and reshape them before the wax hardens.

38 Exhale II
Cotton, 120 × 95cm, 1981.
(Private collection)

For dyeing

Brushes are used extensively in dyeing for painting in individual segments and for all-over background dyeing; this allows more colour selection than immersion dyeing.

The best brushes are made of hair and are tightly packed and absorbent. For small areas a water-colour brush takes up the dye readily and deploys it accurately within the bounds of the wax design. These may range in size and can be used for shading. Some may be cut down to form a short stubble. For ground-colour dyeing use a broader short haired brush which can hold a reserve of dye without it spilling or streaking. A good quality decorating brush up to 13cm (5in.) wide or a foam-backed painting pad would substitute. Avoid overloading the brush.

Dyes penetrate easily, and brushes should therefore be very thoroughly cleaned in a mild detergent and dried after use. If you are using only one brush remember to wash it out thoroughly between colours.

Other applications

In place of brushes, dyes can be painted on with cotton buds in small areas or by means of cotton wool secured by a clothespeg for larger, more expansive fabrics. Sprays can give amazingly subtle effects and range from the compressor to the aerosol or the simple mouth-spray.

Blocks can be made to repeat motifs for waxing. These can be made out of any absorbent or heat-condusive material. Metal, cardboard, felt and pipe-cleaners can all be used: fit them to a block of wood to ensure insulation from the hot wax while printing. The size of the blocks should be limited to a width of 15cm (6in.). Ready-made pastry-cutting shapes make ideal pattern stamps.

COLOUR AND DESIGN

To produce effective colours and integrate them in your design you should fully understand your three variables – fabric, wax and dye – by working in an explorative manner. Observation of the spontaneous interaction between these elements will provide an insight into the nature and characteristics of batik. Certain rules and techniques have to be considered and developed. The dye colour, absorbed by fabric and repelled by resist, is the essential distinctive factor that defines the art of batik. Explore the effects, approach everything innocently and enjoy the experience of applying brush strokes of molten wax. Try out the refined skills of the canting and enjoy applying flowing lines of wax across stretched white cotton. Pour primary dye colours on and see the resist perform. Watch the colours move and flow together, creating spectrums of fresh, unpremeditated pattern.

You will soon appreciate that the waxing effects depend on the tools you employ to wax the fabric. Speed and dexterity will develop with increased experience. You will find, too, that the choice of fabric will influence both the absorption of wax and dye.

Colour

The batik artist delights in a colour language; the educated eye learns to register and perceive a wide spectrum of colour. To use colour in the most effective way it is essential that the artist learns to anticipate the over-dyeing sequences. The first dye-bath determines the direction of the overall colour plan. Dyestuffs each have their own characteristics, depending on the type and skilful use of different effects. These can give added depth and tone to a batik. For instance, reactive dyes cannot always give the intensity that naphthol dyes produce. Produce dye tests on strips of fabric and file these together with the recipes used.

It is useful to know how colour is categorized. There are:

Primary colours — red, yellow and blue, which, when judiciously mixed together, can produce the whole spectrum.

Secondary colours — orange, green and violet. These are made by mixing two primary colours

40 *Measuring jugs, spoons, scales, bowls and baths*
should be of non-reactive materials such as
stainless steel, enamel, Pyrex glass or plastic. When
using chemicals wear a protective mask and rubber
gloves at all times.

(e.g. violet is produced by mixing blue and red).
Intermediate colours — mixtures of primary and secondary colours.
Complimentary colours — opposite colours on the spectrum (e.g. orange and blue).

These terms are used to describe colour character:
Hue — refers to pure colour. The value of colour is altered by the addition of black or white.
Intensity — measured by the amount of light in a colour.

Design

Design is rooted in the real world of observation and it involves a process of selection and emphasis.

You can draw on available sources, but a personal attitude is more valuable and inspirational. Work within your own ability. Try not to be too ambitious at first.

Photographs are a good source of design motifs as they are essentially objects already reduced to flat patterns. Furthermore, framing certain parts of a picture serves to isolate sections and creates strong images. Concentrate on colour, texture and form in isolation from the overall design. When designing with a function in mind, such as for a garment, remember that the pattern or design has to be conceived as part of a three-dimensional form.

Certain attitudes can be established which can fuel your imagination. Keep a sense of yourself; don't slavishly copy; try to grasp the harmony of relationships; sharpen your perception; capitalize on the uniqueness of batik; be exuberant with the technique; and learn also to respect the tools and materials and be confident in your handling of them. Remember, though, that mistakes always happen; don't set yourself goals or rules that subjugate your self-expression. Change and challenge should motivate your concepts.

four
SYNTHETIC DYES

Modern dye chemistry began in 1856 when William Henry Perkin was experimenting with the synthesis of quinine from aniline. By accident he isolated a black tar-like substance, which he discovered contained a colour precipitate. Experimentation produced a purple aniline, referred to subsequently as mauveine or more commonly by the nickname Perkin's purple. Owing to its amazing light- and wash-fastness this coal-tar dye monopolized the dyer's art, despite being very expensive. Rapid experimentation produced brilliant colours, including magenta in 1859, aniline blue in 1860 and the first water-soluble dye in 1862. These synthetic dyes were a great advance on the longer and less predictable dye processes of natural dyestuffs and soon other classes of dyes were discovered: direct dyes in 1884, and synthetic indigo and vat dyes in 1897, which were developed from van Baeyer's work on indigotin. The increasing demand for improved fastness prompted the invention of mordant dyes, including azoic dyes and their various adaptations, which were marketed in the early twentieth century. In 1956 the latest and original chemical type of dye was produced for cotton, called fibre reactive.

Today, petroleum, rather than coal-tar, is used as the basis for the dye in industry. There are innumerable brand names on the market, but in fact only a few companies that produce dyestuffs: ICI in England, Ciba Geigy and Sandoz in Switzerland, Bayer and Hoechst in Germany, and Dupont in France.

DYES SUITABLE FOR BATIK

Dyestuffs suitable for making batik must be capable of being applied to natural fibres in cold water.

To the layman the chemistry may be somewhat formidable and the choice of dyestuffs perplexing, but with clear guidelines colour mixing should be accessible and uninhibiting.

There are six categories of dyestuffs suitable for batik. Directions for making up dyes within the specific class are essentially the same. The categories are:

- fibre-reactive
- naphthol or azoic
- vat
- direct
- acid
- basic

GENERAL DYE THEORY

Most organic fibrous matter absorbs water. If the water contains a colouring, either in a paste or liquid form, it will become attached to the fibre. The intensity of the colour increases as the dyeing process proceeds, transferring it until the dyebath is exhausted. To secure the colour and make it fast and even, compounds, called assistants, are used in the dyebath.

Liquor ratio

To dye the cloth successfully water has to be distributed evenly throughout the cloth. The ratio indicates how much water is required for the dyebath. Most recipes call for a ratio of 30:1. This would indicate that there should be 30 times more water than the dry weight of cloth. A simple calculation would be:

30 × 50g. dry weight of cloth = 1500ml (1.5l) water.

Short dye baths have a low ratio of water to cloth, perhaps as small as 5:1, which would give a high concentration of dye.

Percentage calculation of dye solution

The strength of colour is determined by the ratio of the weight of dye to the volume of water. This percentage is important as it determines both the shade and the fastness of the dyebath. To assess the correct ratio you should keep records of recipes to refer to for accurate results.

A stock solution may make a 5 per cent shade. This would be calculated as follows:

$$\frac{5g.\ dyestuff}{1000ml\ of\ water\ (1l)} = 0.05\ or\ 5\ per\ cent\ colour\ shade$$

Generally 5 per cent would be for a dark shade, whilst 0.5 per cent would be very pale.

FIBRE-REACTIVE DYES

Fibre-reactive dyes were developed by ICI and offer the advantage of simple application combined with a greater degree of light and washing fastness. The brilliant range of colours achieve their fullest intensity on cellulose fibres (particularly mercerized cotton) but may also be used on silk, though with less affinity and diminished absorption.

The reaction is caused by the presence in the dyebath of an alkali that bonds with the actual fibre (i.e. the chemical composition of the fibre alters to form an inseparable compound). If the alkali (soda) is not present then this action does not occur and the colour will wash out. Because the alkali is reacting to the water as well as the cellulose (hydrolysis), the colour deteriorates

and the dyebath has a life of only about four hours. To ensure that the reaction between the dyestuffs and the fibre proceeds effectively it is sufficient to air-dry the cloth for fixation to take place.

Proper control of the factors, together with attention to the rinsing and soaping treatments, will ensure fastness in the wet processes. The most popular dyes in this category are the Procion-M series manufactured by ICI. The H-series is not suitable as these cannot be used cold. Other manufacturers of this class are: Cibacron (Liba/Geigy); Drimarene (Sandoz); Levatix (Bayer) and, Ramazol (Hoechst).

Procion 'M' reactive dyes

Trade colour	Code	Actual colour
Yellow	MX-8G	Brilliant yellow
Yellow	MX-4G	Lemon
Yellow	MX-GR	Golden yellow
Orange	MX-2R	Clear orange
Scarlet	MX-G	Scarlet
Red	MX-5B	Brilliant red
Red	MX-8B	Fuchsia
Rubine	MX-B	Rubine
Navy	MX-RB	Midnight blue
Blue	MX-7RX	Ultramarine violet
Blue	MX-2R	Royal blue
Blue	MX-G	Cerulean
Turquoise	MX-G	Aquamarine turquoise
Brown	MX-GRN	Rust
Brown	MX-3RD	Burnt umber
Olive	MX-3G	Olive green

All the above have 3–4 per cent shade value. There is no black in the Procion range. It can, however, be obtained if you mix three parts navy (MX-RB), one quarter red (MX-5B) and one part yellow (MX-GR). Kenactive, however, produce a ready-made black.

The (equivalent) three primary colours, Red

Temptation *(detail).*
Cotton, 1981.
(Private collection).

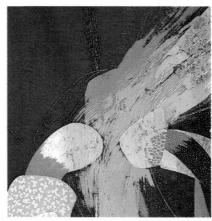

Exhale II *(detail).*
Cotton, 120 x 95 cm, 1981.

**Cotton coat by
Jane Christie.**
Reactive dyes, 1986.

Kimono by Tacy Long.
*Paper, discharge and
reactive dyes,
18 x 18 cm, 1986.*

Life Plant *(detail).*
Cotton, 1981.
(Private collection).

Undercurrent.
Cotton, 120 x 95 cm, 1985.
(Private collection).

Tattooed Lady. *Cotton, naphthol and reactive dyes, 120 x 95 cm, 1983.*

Blue N Dimension by Shigeki Fukumoto.
Cotton, 180 x 170 cm, 1982.

Silk Wall by Norma Starszakowna.
Silk, 270 x 910 cm, 1983. (Commissioned by
General Accident Insurance Co., Perth, Scotland).

MX-8B, Turquoise MX-G and Yellow MX-8G, when mixed give a full spectrum of colour.

Black may have to be applied several times to give a good depth. An alternative is to use the mechanically-bonded naphthol dye for the final colour.

Chemicals

The following elements are used in fibre-reactive dyeing:

Alkali: the alkalis recommended for batik are anhydrous sodium carbonate (soda ash) and sodium bicarbonate. These are the essential fixing agents.

Common table salt: facilitates the penetration and even quality of dyeing and good colour yield.

Urea: synthesized from natural gas, is used as a solubilizing and hydroscopic agent. The dyestuff dissolves more effectively and also delays the chemical reaction with the water by absorbing moisture from the atmosphere. Urea proves an effective ingredient when painting or spraying as it retards the fixing process.

Resist salt L: a mild oxidizing agent which helps to increase colour yield.

Calgon (sodium hexame taphosphate): a water softener that neutralizes any metallic salts which might interfere with the dyeing process. Hard water can cause coagulation with some dyes and thickeners.

Pre-treatment of fabric

The fabric should be thoroughly washed in hot soapy water to remove any sizing or dressing that may prevent dye absorption. Rinse and soak in warm water with 2–4g. of a soap-free detergent – use metapex as a wetting agent – which will open the pores of the fabric. Allow excess water to drip off before immersing in the bath.

Immersion dye recipe

For accurate results the proportions of dyestuff, chemical, fabric and water must be measured, particularly when the exact shade has to be repeated.

Dye bath recipe: 30 × dry weight of cloth (120g. = 1 metre (1yd) fine cotton).
Dye stuff: 0.5–4g. dye to 1 litre dye liquid, depending on shade.
Salt: For 2g. dye – 50g salt to 1 litre dye liquid.
Soda Ash: 10g. to 1 litre dye liquid.

Procedure

(1) Dissolve salt and soda in hot water (140°F (60°C)) in two separate containers (100ml).
(2) Reduce dye powder to a paste of smooth consistency using a small amount of warm water.
(3) Add to dye bath and stir.
(4) Immerse fabric and agitate to ensure thorough penetration.
(5) Add salt solution in three equal portions over 15 minutes. Remove fabric for each addition.
(6) Add soda to dye bath and stir.
(7) Replace fabric for further 45 minutes, turning regularly.
(8) Remove fabric and rinse in cold water.
(9) Air-dry, preferably in humid atmosphere, for at least 2–3 hours.
(10) After removing wax treat fabric to a hot water wash with a mild detergent soap. (2g. Lissapol D soap per litre of water)

Note: once the soda has been added to the dyebath it loses its effectiveness after a few hours. A shorter dyeing method is possible by adding the salt measure in one go and dyeing for less time. However, there is a greater tendency to blotching and streaking with this method. The shade of colour, also, will not be as deep. Handle the waxed fabric with great care in the bath to prevent unnecessary breaks in the resist.

Fast black K-salt procedure

The majority of reactive colours will react with this particular fast salt (diaza) in various shades of brown imitating the soga colour found in Javanese batiks.

(1) Dissolve 4–10g. fast black salt in warm water.
(2) Add 1 litre cold water.
(3) Immerse dry fabric for about five minutes.
(4) Rinse and soap.

Silk or wool dyeing

A very high degree of wet fastness is achieved by chemical linkage to the fibre. It is essential that the silk is degummed before dyeing. In overdyeing the dye sites become occupied after subsequent dyeing when they depend on a chemical type bond. The depth of colour is therefore limited and a mechanically bonded vat or naphthol dye is worth considering for a final dark colour.

For immersion dyeing substitute Glauber's salt for common table salt with half the amount of alkali.

For direct application the above recipe can be used or the acid dye recipe, replacing the alkali (sodium bicarbonate, soda ash) and the resist salt with 2ml acetic acid.

Leave to fix for 24 hours. Rinse and soap, but do not boil.

Direct dye application

For painting, spraying, sponging or splashing techniques, fibre-reactive dyes are applied in a concentrated form. As they are applied directly and not immersed in a bath, the fixation time has to be extended by the use of urea, which helps to delay the dyeing process to allow reaction to occur.

Recipe for chemical water

First prepare a litre of chemical water, which can be stored indefinitely at room temperature.
Dissolve 4–5g. calgon, 140g. urea, 10g. resist salt L in 500ml hot water. Add cold water to make up 1 litre.

Dye recipe and procedure

0.25–3g. dye (depending on colour strength) to 25ml chemical water

0.25g. sodium bicarbonate
Dissolve 1g. soda ash and 0.25g. sodium bicarbonate in a little warm water.

(1) Make up dye powder paste in a little warm water using an amount according to the colour intensity required.
(2) Add required amount of cold chemical water.
(3) Add dissolved alkali just before use.
(4) Apply dye to fabric.
(5) Air dry for at least 12 hours.
(6) Rinse out in running, soapy water.

Note: dry heat, ironing or steaming can all improve fastness. Take care not to overload your colour so that the surface of the fabric becomes powdery.

Pre-treatment of fabric method

Immerse fabric in a solution of soda ash (30g. of soda ash to 1 litre water) for about ten minutes, dry and paint on dye made up with 5g. urea to 100ml water.

Sodium silicate method (water glass)

Mix your dyestuffs with water and paint on the fabric. Let the cloth dry thoroughly. Apply the sodium silicate and spread with an inexpensive brush. Take care to saturate all dyed areas.

Leave for at least one hour and then thoroughly wash out with hot water and soap.

Thickening dye for direct application

In certain instances it may be an advantage to control the spread of the dye solution by adding sodium alginate (Manutex). This is a powder that swells in water and does not react with the dyestuffs and may be removed finally by washing. The thickness is determined by the absorbency of the fabric and dyes used. A thinner solution can be used as a size. Store in an air-tight container in the refrigerator. Procedure is as follows:

(1) Sprinkle 4g. of sodium alginate to a litre of chemical water (recipe on page 66) or proportionately less as it goes a long way.

(2) Stir or mix with an electric blender for several minutes until it has formed an even consistency.

(3) Leave to stand for an hour at least. Stir up before use.

(4) Paste dye powder with thickened chemical water and blend thoroughly.

(5) Apply the dye and leave for 12 hours at least for fixation to occur.

(6) Rinse cloth under warm, running, soapy water.

Fixation of directly applied dyes

Although the natural drying process is perfectly adequate to fix the dyestuffs and fibre, the presence of a warm humid atmosphere can speed up the process. In direct application, when the fabric has to air dry for a long time, the presence of heat and moisture hastens the process. First allow fabric to dry by atmospheric steaming, pressure steaming or steam-baking in an oven, or by simply steam ironing for five minutes. After fixing, rinse in cold running water, ensuring that the fabric is open and the unfixed dye is washed out. Increase the water temperature, soap and boil.

NAPHTHOL OR AZOIC DYES

These dyes produce extremely fast colours by the interaction of two dyebaths. The first bath impregnates the cloth with a chemical and this, in turn, reacts with the dyestuff in the second bath to form an insoluble compound within the fibre. The process is instantaneous, unrivalled for its depth of colour and extremely fast to light, washing and boiling. The entire procedure can

41 Edge
Calico, naphthol-dyed with burnt edge with the wax remaining in the cloth, 170cm long, 1983.

be completed in 15 minutes. Owing to their advantages and their similarity to indigo dyeing techniques, these dyes are the most frequently used in Indonesia. Used originally on cellulose fibres, they give good but somewhat different results on silk and wool. The dyebath lasts approximately six hours, providing it is kept out of direct light.

Naphthol is produced by Hoechst & Bayer. ICI produce a similar dyestuff called Brenthol.

Pre-treatment of fabric
Owing to the instantaneous colour response, it is particularly important to remove all size, starch or processing oils from the fabric before dyeing.

Dye equipment
You will need at least two of everything. Use only non-reactive materials such as plastic, glass, stainless steel or enamel. Small amounts of dye are used in relation to the weight of the fabric. Flat, wide baths are more practical for immersion methods. Measuring by weight is essential because teaspoons give a distorted measurement as the diazo salts weigh about twice as much as naphthol.

Chemicals
Caustic soda (sodium hydroxide) solution is the only chemical required for naphthol dyeing. The solution is prepared by dissolving 441g. caustic soda in 1 litre of cold water. Add the caustic soda carefully, stirring all the time, and make sure you avoid splashes as the solution releases heat and is dangerous. Allow it to cool and put in a dark bottle with either a plastic or cork stopper. Label the bottle clearly and store it in a safe place. If the solution comes into contact with the skin wash immediately in water – the amount used in the dyebath, however, is fractional, and the danger negligible.

Turkey red oil (TRO) or monopol helps to dissolve the naphthol and acts as a wetting agent. As an alternative methylated spirits can be used to reduce the naphthol to a paste.

Dye recipe
The standard proportion by weight of the naphthol to the diazo salts per litre is:
Bath 1: 2g. naphthol to 1 litre water
Bath 2: 4g. diazo salts to 1 litre water
This will give a medium strength colour. For a lighter shade, put 1g. naphthol in 1 litre of water in bath 1, followed by 2g. diazols salts in 1 litre of water in bath 2. For a darker shade, put 2g. naphthol in 1 litre of water in bath 1, followed by 6g. diazo salts in 1 litre g. water in bath 2.

There is a coded range of naphthol and a wide range of colour salts. By using the same base with a variety of colour salts or different bases with one colour salt, a vast range of colours can be achieved. It is sufficient, however, to begin with just two or three of each. Individual recipes and preferences will result from your experimenting.

Preparation of napthol bath

(1) Make a paste from 2g. naphthol with monopol or TRO in a measuring cup and work to a smooth consistency. Alternatively, use a little methylated spirit instead of monopol or TRO.

(2) Add 25ml boiling water and stir the solution, making certain the chemical has completely dissolved.

(3) Immediately add 5–20ml caustic soda solution (441g. caustic soda in 1 litre water). Stir drop by drop until the naphthol becomes clear and yellow, but use no more than is absolutely necessary.

(4) Leave the cool solution for a few minutes.

(5) Add cold water to make the mixture up to 1 litre.

Note: if the naphthol does not clear when the caustic solution is added, reheat and stir.

Preparation of diazo salt bath

(1) Measure out 4g. diazo salt.

(2) Mix to a paste with cold water.

(3) Add cold water to make up to 1 litre.

Procedure for dyeing

(1) Place the wet fabric in the naphthol bath. It is essential that the whole fabric is impregnated for about five minutes.

(2) Lift out and allow all the excess naphthol to drip back into the bath. Hang for at least ten minutes – longer for heavier fabric.

(3) Submerge the fabric in the diazo salt bath. The colour will develop immediately on contact. Agitate the fabric and leave for five minutes or until there is no further colour change. Too rapid removal will result in a loss of rub-fastness. Hang out until it is drip-free.

(4) Rinse in running cold water until clear.

(5) Soap and boil the fabric to eliminate excess dye and to stabilize the colour.

Note: keep the two dye-baths well apart. An excess of naphthol in the diazo salt bath exhausts the colour. In order to increase colour intensity repeat this process, rinsing off each time after the second bath.

Intermediate salt bath
After removing the fabric from the naphthol bath a quick rinse in a salt bath (3g. salt to 1 litre cold water) will remove the excess chemical and facilitate the dyeing process. This, however, is optional.

Direct application by brushing
Both naphthol and colour salts can be applied manually by brush or spray techniques. A thickener can be used for painting. This application offers considerable freedom, owing to the highly sensitive reaction between naphthol and colour salts in combination. Because the dyeing process involves two stages, how accurately you predict the finished colour depends very much on experience.

Direct application of diazo colour salts

(1) First wet the fabric, then immerse in the naphthol. Hang the fabric out to dry away from direct sunlight.

(2) Spray or paint the fabric with a concentrated solution of colour salts (2g. to 125ml water).

(3) Dry out thoroughly to ensure complete coupling and prevent 'bleeding' in the washing off process (4ml soap with 2g. washing soda in a litre of hot water).

Scour away any loose dye particles after developing. Particularly interesting effects can be obtained by spraying as the colour salts react on the naphthol, each colour separating out as they do not overdye.

Direct application of naphthol
Apply the naphthol in concentrated form:

(1) Make a paste with 2g. naphthol.
(2) Add 50ml boiling water.
(3) Add caustic solution.
(4) Top up to 125ml cold water.
(5) Apply naphthol.
(6) Dry before immersing in a colour salt bath. The salts are very soluble in water and will wash out of the concentrated parts of the fabric with a thorough washing.

Note: when painting on naphthol do not use a fine natural bristle or hair brush as the soda content will corrode it.

Direct application of naphthol and diazo colour salts
Use the two previous direct recipes and wash the fabric to remove loose dye particles. The result can be a little unpredictable as some of the colour salts are not compatible with these methods and vary in their developing time.

Dyeing notes

- Naphthol will react with diazo salts to produce colour.
- Never mix the naphthol with diazo salt.

- Any combination of naphthols can be mixed together, as can any combination of diazo salts.
- Measure by weight, not volume.
- Keep a record of samples of resulting colours.
- The method of dyeing is different from that employed with other dyes; the fabric action is 'passing through' the bath. The fabric does not have to be completely immersed for a set time.
- Even quality of colour comes with experience and dexterity. Speed is essential for the dyeing action as colour develops instantly.

Colour mixing

Naphthols have a colour spectrum ranging from intense black to subtle hues, all dependent on the proportion of naphthol to diazo salt in equal amounts of water. Shades can be produced by varying the proportion of naphthol to diazo salt. Never mix the two together. For a general indication of colour note the following essential naphthols and their coding:

Naphthol AS/AS D   develops as colour salt
Naphthol LB   develops brown values
Naphthol G   develops yellow values
Naphthol TR   develops pastel colours
Naphthol BO   develops strongest colour value
Naphthol GR   develops green with blue salts

Naphthol BS, SR, OL all vary slightly.
The strongest salts are Red B, Blue BB, Black K, BTL and ANS. Other colours are: Scarlet GG, Blue B, Violet B, Bordeaux GP, Orange RD, Green BB, Yellow GC.

Proportions for recipes 2g. naphthol – 4g. colour salt to a litre of water.

As an example if you use naphthol G with Red B diazo salts you develop a golden yellow. Used with LB the same salt gives a red-brown.

AS BO + Scarlet develops clear red;

AS BO + Red B develops maroon;
AS G + Blue BB develops ochre;
AS G + Red B develops golden yellow;
AS LB + Yellow GC develops pale brown;
AS LB + Red B develops red brown;
AS + Blue BB develops royal blue;
AS + Red B develops light crimson.

A deep black develops if you increase the proportion 2:8 using ASBO and Black ANS. Re-dip if necessary to increase depth.

It is possible to mix naphthols: for example, for brown, mix ½g. AS D with 1½g. AS G using Bordeaux GB.

For green, mix ½g. AS D with 1½g. AS G using Blue BB.

On silk similar colours can be obtained by the use of vinegar or acetic acid in the diazo salt bath. Use approximately 2ml to 1 litre water.

Note: a standard recipe is 2g. naphthol and 4g. colour salt to 1 litre of water. Lighter shades would be 0.5–1g. to 1 litre. For darker shades use considerably more. Only testing with different proportions will give you the benefit of the full range of colour.

Patchy dyeing

Patchy naphthol dyeing is a common problem, which can be remedied. There are several possible causes:

- The cloth has not been wetted before immersion.
- The cloth has not passed through the dye baths thoroughly and been impregnated equally. Unlike other dyes the cloth has a short developing time and does not have to be totally immersed for a specific length of time as the reaction occurs instantly within the fibre.
- The colour salts are exhausted. Remedy this by draining out the excess naphthol solution in the cloth by rinsing in a salt bath before immersing in the colour salt bath. The intermediary stage extends the life of the

colour salt bath by fixing the naphthol in the cloth.

VAT DYES

These are unique in that they are insoluble in water and have no affinity with the fibre until they are reduced to a soluble form by an alkali solution. They are used primarily on cotton, although they can be used on silk and are extremely fast to light and washing – in fact the fastest. The dye will appear colourless until exposed to oxidizing agents which develop the colour.

Indigosol dyes are the most suitable for batik as they are derived from the indigo vat principle. They have a range of bright colours which can be developed by light and heat or by a bath of hydrochloric acid solution.

To apply the solution is simple and rapid, either by immersion or direct application. Two baths are necessary: the first contains the indigosol dye, the second the developing solution.

Procedure

(1) Make a paste with the dyestuff and hot water, using 2–3g. per litre of water.
(2) Immerse the wetted fabric briefly. Hang out until excess is drained off.
(3) Immerse in second bath containing 15ml of hydrochloric acid and 1g. sodium nitrate per litre of cold water to develop colour. Beware of inhaling the fumes. It is a good idea to wear a face mask.
(4) Lay the cloth out in the sun to develop the colour, turning the cloth for a few minutes (if cloudy about 15 minutes). Keep it away from shadows. Then draw the cloth through the acid bath.
(5) Rinse out the hydrochloric acid from the cloth thoroughly washing it in cold water. For a deeper colour repeat the process. For certain colours the sodium nitrate is added to the dyebath and can be exposed to

sunlight as well as further development in the second bath.

Note: the acid treatment should not be unduly prolonged because of the possibility of damage to the fabric.

Direct colour application with indigosol

The dye solution can be made up in a concentration of 2g. dyestuff to 50ml water. A brush, sponge or spray can be used. Apply the dye to both sides of the cloth and allow it to dry. Draw the cloth through the acid bath and rinse it out to ensure that the acid treatment doesn't damage the fabric.

This method of brushing indigosol dyes is used in the Pekalongan area of Java.

DIRECT OR APPLICATION DYES

These dyestuffs have a direct affinity with cellulose fibres and the acid levelling class and can be used for silk. They work best in a dyebath of 185–194°F (85–90°C), but naturally have to be cooled for use in batik. They are so named because they don't need a mordant and are easy to apply. However, they do not possess good wash-fastness, but can be improved by after-treatment with recommended fixatives. The most common brand is Deka L, which is a union of the direct and acid components.

These dyes are soluble in water and can be freely mixed. They have the advantage of having a brilliant range of colours including a good black with an unlimited array of hues. They are excellent for discharge, and once used they can be stored and reused.

Procedure

(1) Make a paste mixing 10–20g. with warm water.
(2) Add 1 litre water and bring to the boil.
(3) Dissolve ten times the amount of salt to dye powder.
(4) Add to the dyebath.

(5)   Leave the solution to cool.
(6)   Immerse the fabric for 30–45 minutes.
(7)   Rinse the fabric.

For dyeing silk or wool replace salt with white vinegar or acetic acid. Steaming is generally required to fix the colour.

ACID DYES

These dyestuffs have a direct affinity with protein fibres, such as silk or wool. They are economical to use and have a range of vibrant colours, although they are not wash-fast. They should always be dry-cleaned.

Acids are used as dyeing assistants. For the craft dyer acetic acid or white vinegar is recommended, although ammonium sulphate as an acid donor is more of a guarantee against streaking, as it slows the dyeing process down. Pre-metalized dyestuffs are similar to acid, but are exceptionally resistant to fading and yield intense colour. Both types of dyes require steaming for colour fixation.

Use a similar dyeing procedure as the direct dyes (see p. 00), but use acetic acid or Glauber's salt.

BASIC DYES

This group comprises a number of dyes that can be applied to silk and wool. A mordant is needed for cotton. These basic dyes were the first synthetic dyes made from coal-tar derivatives. They have an organic colour base soluble in an acid solution. They are bright colours with poor fastness and are rarely used in industrial dyeing today, but are economical and easy to use for the craft dyer. Their washfastness can be improved with treatment in tannic acid but this has the effect of subduing the colour. The fabric should be dry-cleaned. Tinfix, manufactured by Sennelier, is a well-known batik dye.

Procedure

(1)   Make a paste with 0.5–1g. dyestuff to one teaspoon of acetic acid (or manufacturer's fixative).
(2)   Add 250ml hot water and stir.
(3)   Top up with 750ml tepid water.
(4)   Immerse the fabric for 30–40 minutes.
(5)   Rinse the fabric.

DISCHARGE DYEING OR BLEACHING

Discharging is a chemical process to remove colour from a previously dyed fabric. This method of removing colour from the unwaxed areas offers you a radical opportunity to reappraise and change colours whilst the work is in progress. All dyes are dischargable to a lesser or greater extent, depending on the strength of the chemicals used. However, because of their fastness some reactive and naphthol colours are more resistant. Household bleach can be used on cotton providing it is sufficiently diluted to ensure that the chlorine does not destroy the fibres. Dilute bleach from 3–10 times with cold water depending on shade required. Test it before putting the actual work into the bleaching solution. A more concentrated solution is used for spraying effects. Place the fabric in a bath and agitate, ensuring complete evenness for about ten minutes. Rinse thoroughly, adding a neutralizer, (2g. to 1 litre water of acetic acid or vinegar). The rinsing is to stop any further damage to the fibres.

An alternative and more reliable procedure is to make a discharge solution as follows:

(1)   Add 30g. potassium permanganate to one litre of water.
(2)   Add 2.50ml hydrochloric acid.
(3)   Totally immerse the cloth until all the colour has discharged – five minutes approximately.

42 Hot bath
Cotton reactive-dyed 120 × 95cm, 1982.
(Private collection)

(4)   Neutralize a solution of 50g. sodium hydrosulphite in 2 litres of water.
(5)   Wash cloth through for a couple of minutes.
(6)   Rinse and dry.

Caution: these chemicals are extremely dangerous. Wear rubber gloves, washing them in water after each procedure. Do not inhale fumes. If any chemicals touch your skin wash immediately in plenty of running water. Protect your eyes by wearing safety goggles and ensure that rubber gloves are strong and not porous or damaged.

STEAMING AND FIXING METHODS

The procedure varies according to the dye used. With naphthol, reactive and vat dyed fabrics steaming is generally not required. With direct and acid dyes steaming is usually necessary. A number of liquid and powdered fixers are sometimes recommended by the manufacturers.

During steaming, heat and moisture combine to promote a permanent bond between the dye and the fibre. Before proceeding break off loose wax and iron out between absorbent paper. Paste or gutta evaporates during the steaming process.

Improvised vessels large enough to contain the wrapped fabric can be prepared as follows:

(1)   Set a wire rack 10cm high on the bottom of the container.
(2)   Fill with water to below platform level.
(3)   Place a layer of newspaper or cloth on the rack.
(4)   Boil the water.
(5)   Place unprinted paper or lining paper on the fabric back and front, fold it concertina style or coil and tie it with string. Keep away from the side of the container.

(6)   Place wrapped fabric on platform and cover with a pad of newspaper or cloth to protect the fabric from condensation or suspend the bundle from a stick placed across the top of the container.
(7)   Place a thick pad over the opening and put the lid on. Weight the lid down to build up the pressure, but not so tight that it prevents the steam from escaping.
(8)   Bring the water to the boil and steam for 30 minutes to two hours, depending on the size and weight of the fabric. Add more water if it evaporates as it is the balance of the moisture and heat that is important.
(9)   Remove the fabric and untie it, making sure none of the condensation falls on the fabric.

FINISHING

Rinse the fabric in running water and agitate it so that the excess dye is washed away and does not stain the fabric. Soap out with warm water.

Some dyes can be made more colourfast by a prescribed fixative, particularly for acid or direct dyes.

Final step

Dry the fabric, but do not wring it out or twist it to remove the moisture. Finish it by ironing while it is still damp.

Other fixing methods you might test are:

● ironing with a warm steam iron.
● air dry in warm, humid atmosphere for a day. Under the right condition the dye will set. If it is too moist the colour will run. If too dry, the powder will remain on the surface without penetrating and will partly wash out in the rinsing.
● dry-bake wrapped in oven for five minutes at 141°C (285°F).

five
PROJECTS

Project one: combining techniques with creative responses

43 I am drawing my design onto the cotton using a 4B pencil and drawing instruments. The drawing is simply a device to guide me through the initial processes of waxing and dyeing, whilst giving me plenty of latitude for creative manoeuvre as the work progresses.

44 For spraying within a defined area a stencil is cut and fixed in the correct position with masking tape to ensure that the edges do not lift during the spraying process. An adhesive vinyl is an ideal alternative. Carry the work out on a firm table.

45 A mouth spray provides an effective and economic means of creating soft and undulating textures. A minimal amount of dye is needed. It should be a dense colour, blown sparingly so that the effect is crisp. If you over-spray the dye will become flat and undermine the stencil. Additional colours can be sprayed on providing the previous colour has dried first. After drying, remove the stencil carefully. You might wish to use it again, perhaps in another position. Any amount of further spraying can be applied providing that you respect the correct dye procedures. Allow time to fix.

46 Here, the fabric is stretched onto a frame with
drawing pins. Pull tightly without causing any
distortion on the weave. Posture and position are
checked to ensure a comfortable and accessible
working distance from my wax source. Proceed to
cover the already sprayed area (providing it has
been fixed) and white portions of the design. Some
areas are treated with cooler wax to register the
subtle strokes of the brush. Other areas are solidly
retained by a hotter, more penetrating wax
application, with further layers to follow
immediately.

47 *The strength of the wax resistance can vary, becoming only apparent when the cloth is dyed. The ultimate response cannot be anticipated, and only when the cloth is free of wax can it really be judged.*

At this stage the fabric has been waxed and dyed. The excess dye has been washed out after fixing, and the fabric has been immersed in boiling water to remove wax. You can now enclose areas again with wax. Note that interim wax removal

gives you the opportunity of having unrelated colour progressions with overdyeing. For instance, you can preserve the green with wax whilst leaving the white to take a red dye. It is a very exciting way to work as vivid colour relations can be assured. The process of removing the wax offers a different colour prospect each time. In the direct wax and overdyeing method, superimposing opposite colours will result in neutrals because, by nature, the dyes are transparent.

48 Small amounts of dye colour are painted on
with a brush; allow them to fuse with each other.
They are restrained only by the waxed areas.
Fibre-reactive dyes can be applied liberally,
bleeding and mixing with amazing freedom. The
main advantage of applying local brushed areas of
colour is to have a strikingly multicoloured ground
to put wax on. Judgement and anticipation of the
brushed colour flow is vital to achieve successful
integration of different types of dye applications.

49 *After another immersion dyeing the wax imagery gradually evolves. Holding the canting very lightly, work fine chevron marks over the previously waxed and dyed areas to retain them before redyeing in a darker colour. Progressing through the work, juxtapose canting skills with intuitive brush strokes to act as a counterpoint to enliven with line and texture.*

50 It is important not to crush the work and so the container must be large enough to ensure that the dye penetrates the fabric evenly. Unintentional cracking of the wax resist at this stage may impair the design. Therefore it is vital to take care in handling the cloth.

51 The low, wide container allows the fabric to absorb the colour without crushing the fabric or causing uneven dyeing. Gentle moving of the bath exposes all parts to the dye without you having to handle the brittle wax surfaces. Note how totally the wax resists.

52 *All colours and forms are contained under the wax with the exception of the background, which is the only part exposed to the successive colours.*

Project two: overdyeing technique with reactive dyes

*53 Prepare the design and colour scheme on paper.
Test that the fabric has been pre-treated and has
no starch that will react with the dye. Transfer the
design on to the fabric by tracing it directly
through, if necessary with the aid of a light box.*

*Molten wax can easily collect on the outside of
the bowl of the canting and will hinder the even
flow from the spout when you least expect it. Try
to get into the habit of using an absorbent paper
towel in the cup of your hand to prevent any
accident occuring. Wipe the bowl thoroughly after
each refilling.*

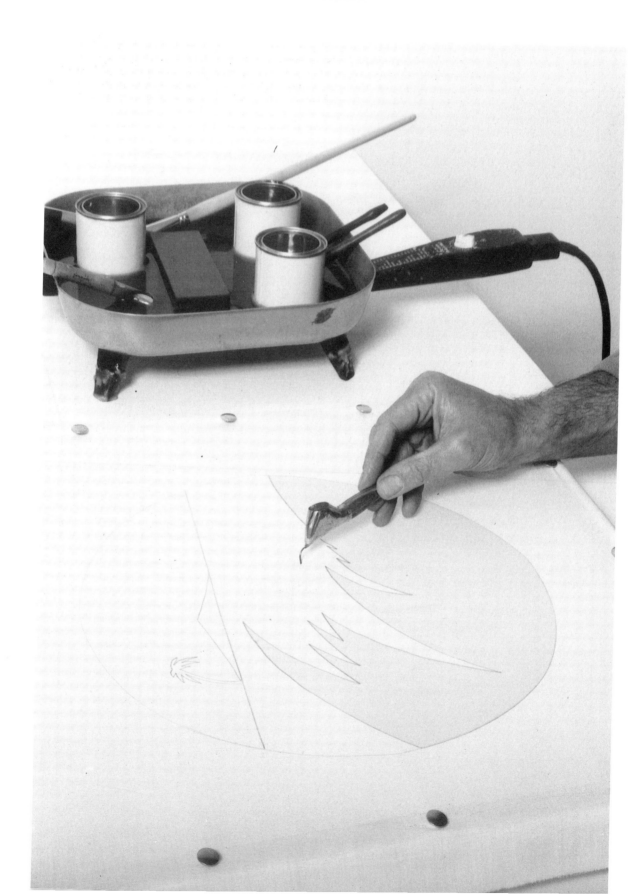

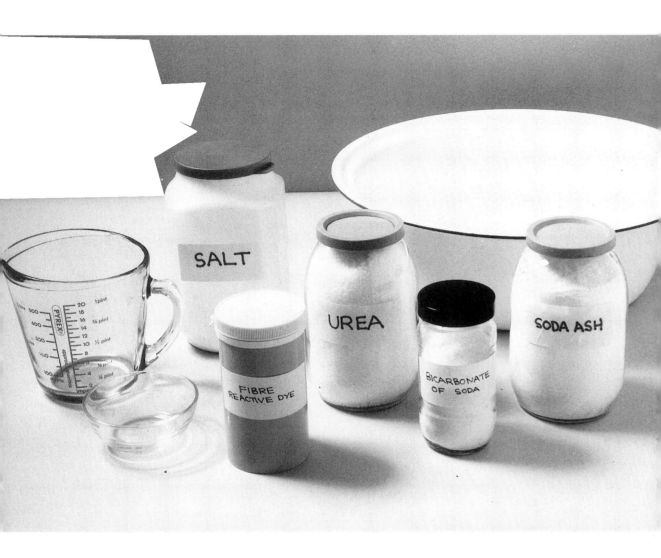

54 Apply wax to the areas that will remain white. The waves are already waxed. The canting adds some sparkle in the form of dots. Note that the electric frying pan holds a number of different recipes of wax in separate containers. The wax is only a few centimetres deep. A weight is set in the wax to act as a rest for the cantings.

55 Prepare the first dye bath of light blue reactive dye with the chemicals illustrated. You will find a full explanation of the recipes and procedure on page oo.

56 Paste up the dye stuff in a little warm water. Be
sure to dissolve it completely before topping up
with cold water. In the undissolved state the
dyestuff has no affinity with the fibre – adding
water activates it.

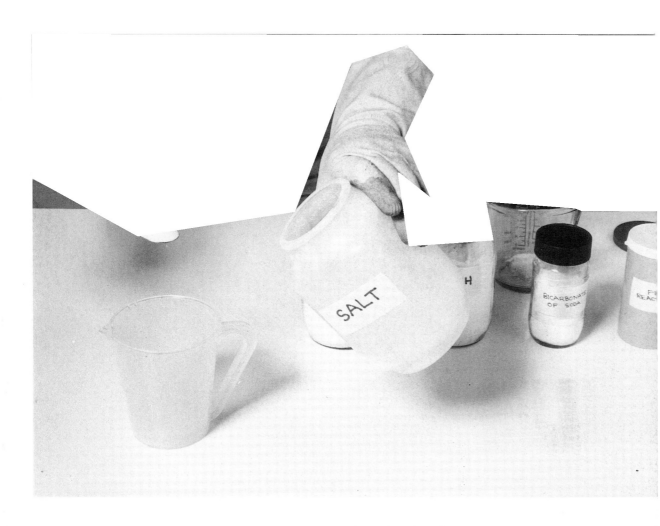

57 Preparing the salt.

58 *Dissolving the soda ash.*

59 *Making up your dyebath. Place the fabric in the bath and add the salt solution in three stages. Remove the fabric after 15 minutes and add the dissolved soda. Dye for a further 45 minutes whilst agitating the solution.*

60 On the second waxing on blue the canting waxes around the more involved shapes of the tree, guided by the pencil line. My grip is fairly relaxed, with a finger acting as a stabilizer on the fabric. Adjust the frame to the most accessible working position.

61 Use the brush for waxing up to the canting line and filling in the sky. Don't overload the brush with wax. Obtain a measure of the flow before committing yourself to a definite line.

62 *The second and final dip in navy blue. Any marbling texture is created by crushing, discriminately, the wax surfaces before immersion in the dye bath.*

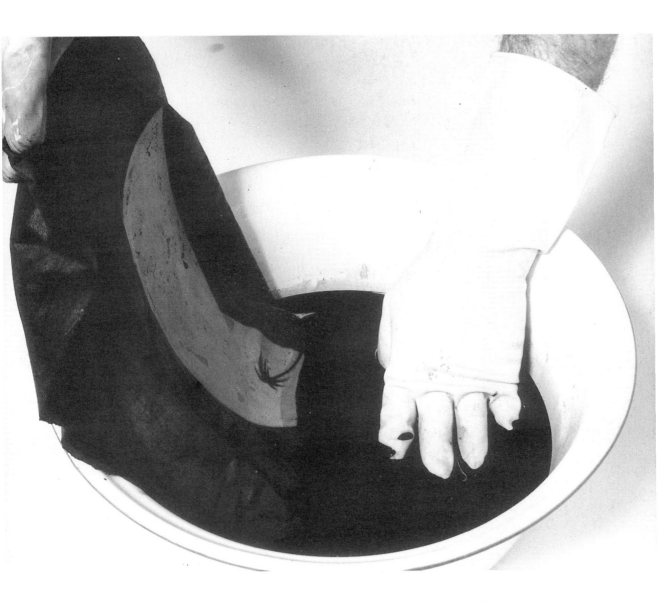

63 Move the waxed fabric through the dye to
ensure complete penetration. An economic measure
of dye solution can be made, providing that you
turn the fabric continually in the bath.

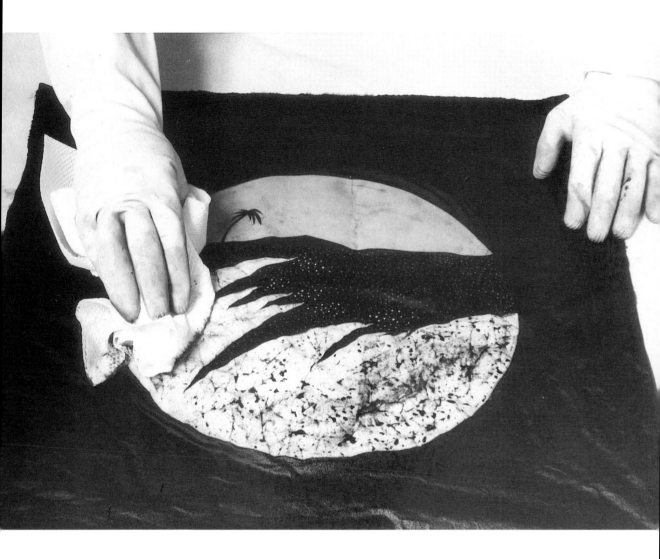

64 *Remove the fabric from the bath and quickly clean any dye off the wax surfaces with absorbent paper.*

65 *After drying the fabric most of the wax can be removed by ironing. Place the material between layers of newsprint and replace the saturated paper with fresh layers until most of the wax is absorbed. Remove the paper whilst the wax is still molten so that the paper does not stick to the fabric.*

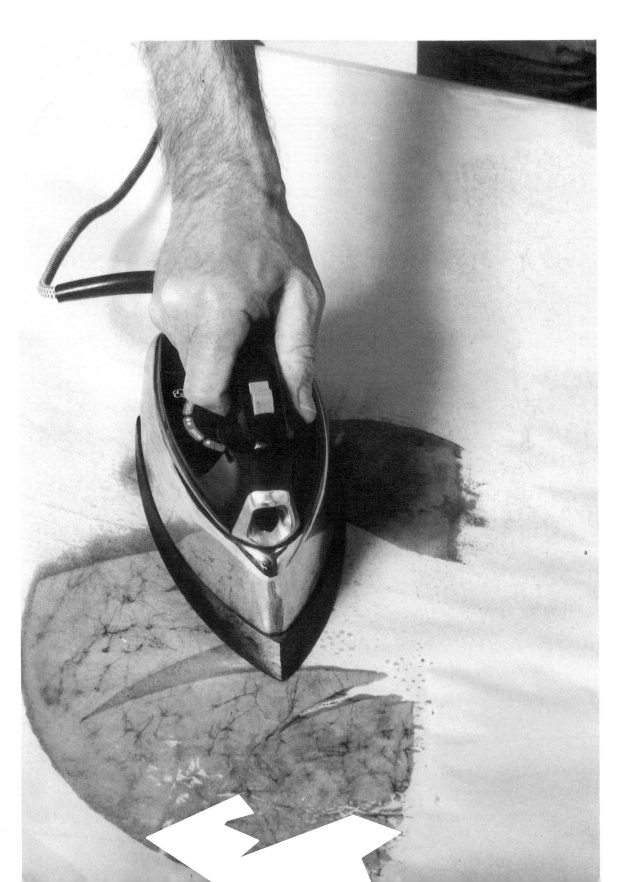

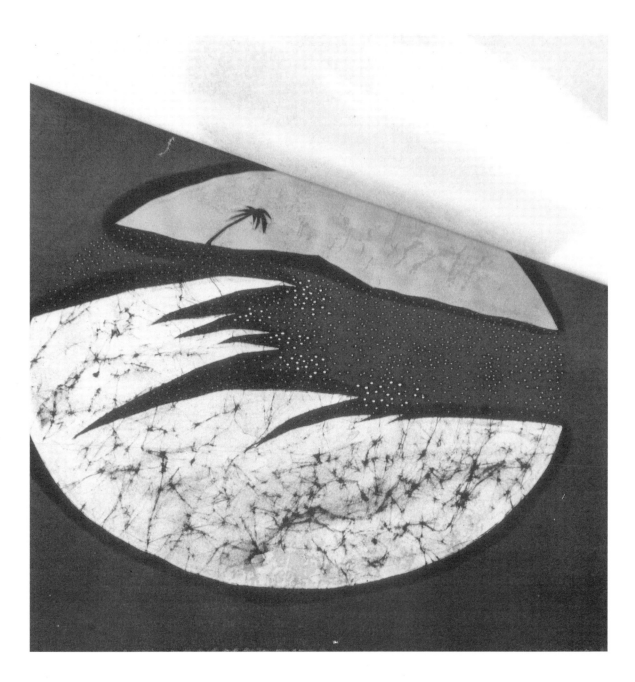

66 *Repeat the ironing process. Replace clean paper on both sides of the fabric. To remove the remaining wax completely, you must dry clean the fabric. When using cleaning solvents, such as fine petrol or white spirit, take care as they are flammable. Finally, rinse the fabric in cold water and then wash in a hot solution of soap detergent such as Metapex, using 3g. to a litre of water. Rinse, dry and iron. The detergent will remove the loose colour and any cleaning fluid that might interfere with the natural 'handle' and fastness of the fabric.*

Project three: wax removal between dyeing using naphthol or azoic dyes

67 Paint broad brush strokes of wax onto a white ground.

68 Use an Indonesian canting with four spouts to make parallel lines. After filling with hot wax the flow may be too rapid and the lines will converge. Wait a few seconds for the wax to cool a little and then test on paper.

69 A Chinese or Japanese sumi-style brush is ideal for waxing a lively and rhythmic line. It has the advantage of a fine tip with a flexible and full body which acts as a reservoir for the wax. It is advisable not to leave these brushes in the wax pots as this distorts their shape.

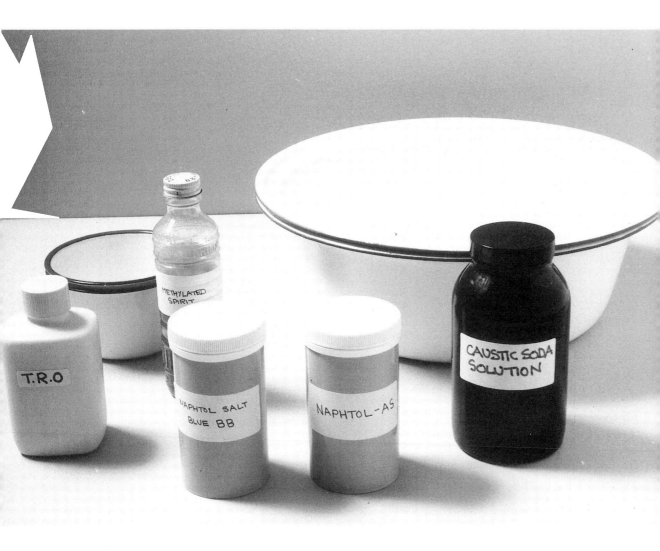

*70 Naphthols are a two-stage dyeing procedure.
The first is a colourless naphthol solution, the
second a fast-colour salt which develops the
colour.*

71 In preparing dyebaths and chemicals it is
imperative that the equipment and the work top
are clean. A full description of the recipes and
procedure is on page 66–70.

72 *Measure the naphthol out by weight: a ratio of*
one measure of naphthol to two of colour salt,
depending on the strength of colour you require.

73 *Paste the naphthol with a little methylated*
spirit, monopol or turkey red oil (sulphonated
castor oil) which help to dissolve it. Add boiling
water.

74 Add a solution of caustic soda. Stir and the solution changes its composition and becomes a clear yellow colour. If, on adding the alkali, there is no change, re-boil the solution. Add it to a litre of cold water.

75 Measure and paste the colour-fast salt with some warm water.

76 Top up with cold water equal in amount to the first bath. The bath on the left contains the naphthol solution, the second bath the fast colour salt.

77 The waxed cloth is put into the naphthol bowl. Take care to ensure all over penetration of the solution. Remove the cloth and allow the solution to drip off. If excess naphthol is not removed from the fabric it acts as a barrier to the colour salt, preventing it from penetrating the fabric.

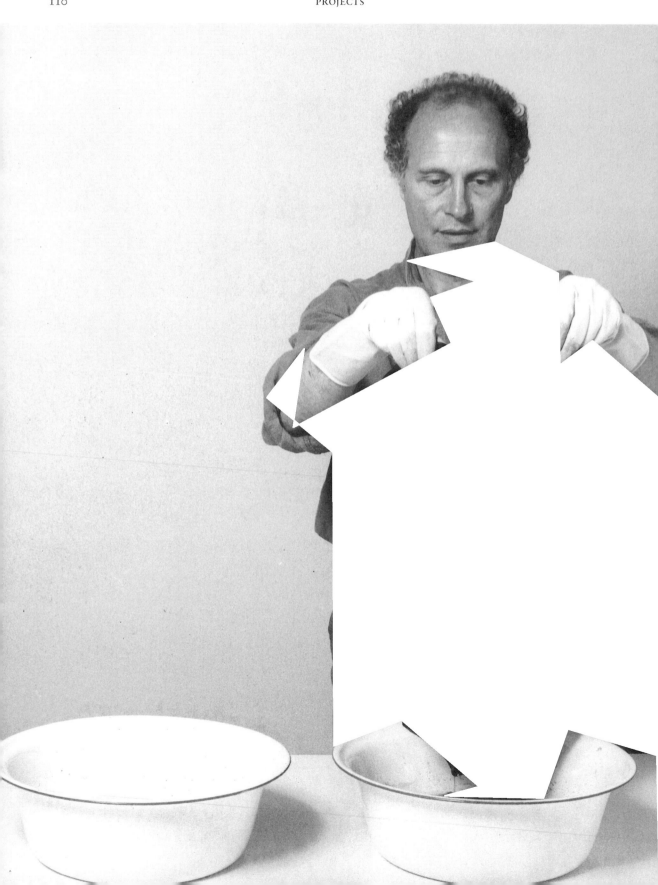

79 *The removal of the wax by boiling out. Fill a suitable container with water and bring to the boil. Add two tablespoons of soda. Break off as much wax from the fabric as possible and submerge for about ten minutes. Stir vigorously and then place the batik in cold water. Any wax remnants solidify at once and can be removed easily from the surface. Wash in hot soapy water and rinse. Repeat the process again if necessary. Silk should not be brought to boiling point. The appearance of the washed silk may be improved by the addition of acetic acid, lemon juice or vinegar. Don't empty hot waxed water down the drain. Leave it to cool and remove wax, then dispose of the water. The re-use of wax is not recommended as the adhesive qualities will have been exhausted during the boiling-out process.*

78 *Draw the naphtholated cloth through the salt bath and the colour will develop instantly. Avoid exposing the dyebath to light. Turn for about five minutes and then hang for ten minutes. Rinse and soap the cloth in hot water. Fixing is immediate and does not require any special drying or steaming facility. If, on re-using, the salt solution becomes turgid, add a little acetic acid.*

80 Re-waxing upon the wax-free batik. Reserve the canting lines of wax on the white and first colour grounds.

81 Second dip colour.

82 *Waxing before the final dip. The great advantage of removing wax between colour dips is that it enables you to start afresh. It is possible to over-dye the exposed colours whilst rewaxing parts of the original design. This method extends the scope of the dyer, increasing both the depth and subtlety of the colour balances.*

Project four: direct dye application

83 A drawing is traced onto the silk. A fine wax line encompasses the forms. Examine the back of the fabric to check that the wax has penetrated through and there are no gaps in the lines so that the colour can't escape. These barriers can be done more boldly with a brush.

In brush dyeing there are three basic techniques: fill-in colour of individual segments; all-over brushing; and applying shading on an already dyed ground.

The most receptive brushes to use are made of deer hair. The size would depend on the desired effect and distribution of dye. Fill the brush with dye, taking undue excess out before applying it to the silk. Brush quickly, overlapping when joining the colour. Be cautious about painting too close to the wax barrier. The colour spreads without too much assistance. The colour when dry becomes subdued and may need more than one application to increase the depth. To give dimension to the design, shading and accents can be added over the ground colour. A small amount of dye is applied first. A second dry brush rubbed onto the wet edge softens and graduates the shading into the background.

Further waxing and subsequent brush application of dye can build up the structure.

84 Gateway II
Calico, naphthol, stencilled and wax-sprayed,
pleated, 170 × 170cm, 1980.

Project five: stencilling

85 Cut the design out of adhesive vinyl or foil.

86 Remove the paper layer and stick firmly to fabric. Pin onto the frame.

87 Take a large firm brush and fill with molten wax. Take the excess out and test for stipple on paper. The distribution should be fine and even. Transfer to the fabric area using rhythmic, brisk flicks of the brush. To register the stipple pattern it should be fairly dense and restricted to the open forms in the stencil. For finer spray use the bowl of a spoon to flip the brush, or simply tap the handle.

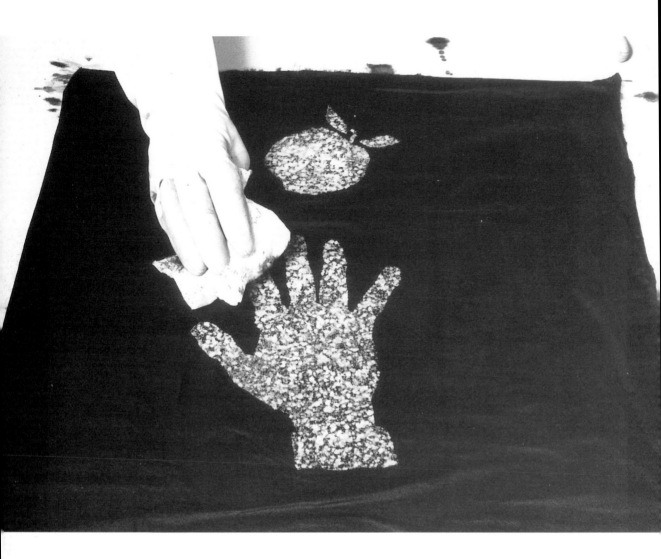

88 The stencil has been removed and the fabric dipped. The textured wax form of the hand and apple have resisted the effect of the colour. Multiple stencils and dye sequences can build up subtle blendings, independently or in combination with other techniques. For brushing directly onto cloth, use a low temperature and firm wax to retain the exact stencil edge.

Project six: etching wax – sgraffito

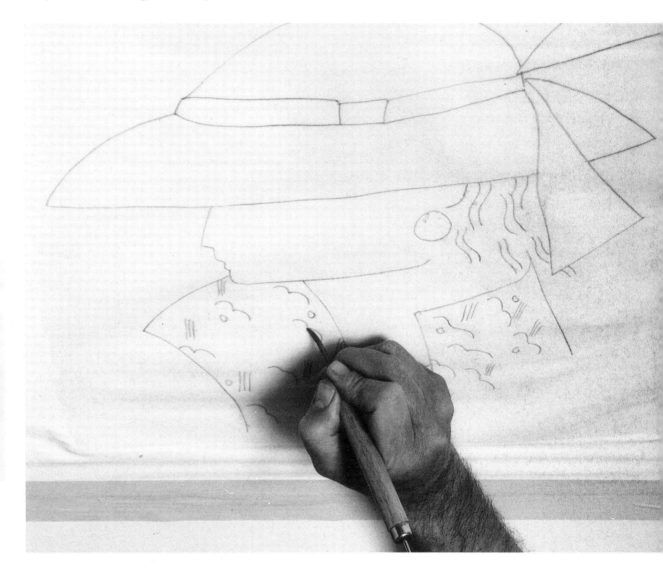

89 Draw the design on to fabric and tape it firmly down to a plastic or glass base. Take a large brush full of wax and spread evenly over the whole fabric, using a non-cracking recipe of wax. Use a tool with a dull metal point to avoid damaging the cloth. Using a firm hand, draw the tool towards you removing a line of wax and so exposing the fabric. For clearer definition repeat on the reverse side. This produces a linear drawing, but further scraping and cross-hatching can add textural variety and interest.

*90 The etched line in the wax is exposed to the
dark dye bath. The colour penetrating to the
fabric. This is a reverse of the conventional
'negative/positive' batik approach, and is
particularly useful in sharpening up areas that have
lost their form. Take care to restrict any
distracting veining in the wax surface. This
technique produces controlled hair-lines; various
tools produce a range of etched effects which open
the cloth to the dye.*

Project seven: wax printing

91 Providing the stamp is made of a material that is both absorbent and a good conductor of heat, a range of stamps can be made to repeat patterns in wax. Metal strips, pipe cleaners and nails fixed to a wooden block can be made into sophisticated designs. Ready-made stamps such as biscuit cutters, corks or matchboxes give definitive shapes.

Lay the cloth on plastic sheeting with a soft underlay, hold the stamp in a shallow wax pot for a few seconds, raise it and tap the excess wax off gently and place it firmly on the cloth. Register the pattern and release. Refuel and repeat the pattern.

92 *For textural qualities, pad on any surface that will absorb the wax and transfer the stamp to cloth. The effect can be swamped by using an excess of wax. Practise and get the measure of this before committing the texture to cloth. The fine indentations of this paper towel can be captured, adding qualities that are distinctly different from using conventional tools.*

six

FURTHER EFFECTS WITH WAXING

93 Stencilled Pattern by Irene Kent
*Cotton, reactive-dyed, stencil and brushed wax,
90 × 100cm, 1985.*

If you experiment with materials, tools and textures you can often produce richly decorated batiks. The following are suggestions for increasing the expressive vocabulary of batik:

- try working with coarse and textured fabrics. Although the control of the wax and the degree of penetration is difficult to master, the response on a velvet or towelling surface is richly rewarding.
- lightly dampen the fabric before waxing. This results in a very fragile resist that creates a unique crackle and soft gossamer effect when dyed.
- submerge wax cloths in cold water to harden the wax to obtain precise marbling in dyeing.
- warm the wax or melt it with an iron to obtain partial absorption of dye and no cracked effect.
- fold and press waxed cloths to cause parallel lines in dip-dyeing.
- place the fabric on textured surfaces or objects such as rough wood or corrugated card. Brush the wax on. Dye, and the transferred textured effects will then become apparent on the fabric.
- double-fold the fabric and wax through both parts. The underside will be a slightly ghosted version of the top cloth.
- paper is an alternative material to cloth. Use a strongly structured, absorbent paper. Place the paper on a glass or plastic surface and wax. Watercolours, inks or dyes can be brushed on. Dipping would dissolve and damage the paper unless it was particularly strong. Remove the wax by ironing out between sheets of newsprint. Re-wax the whole if you don't want the design to be marred by the wax pressed edge – this gives a more harmonious effect and strengthens the paper which then can be cut or folded and used as collage. Using paper is an excellent method for a beginner to experiment upon.
- leather and wood also have exciting possibilities.

94 Six Fold
Paper, naphthol-dyed, 86 × 56cm, 1980.

TECHNICAL VARIATIONS TO EXPLORE

- To comprehend the 'negative' concept of batik, draw a wax composition on a white ground and dye black. Be sensitive in applying wax, particularly to the handle and quality of application. Greater emphasis on these factors will enliven the result. The more

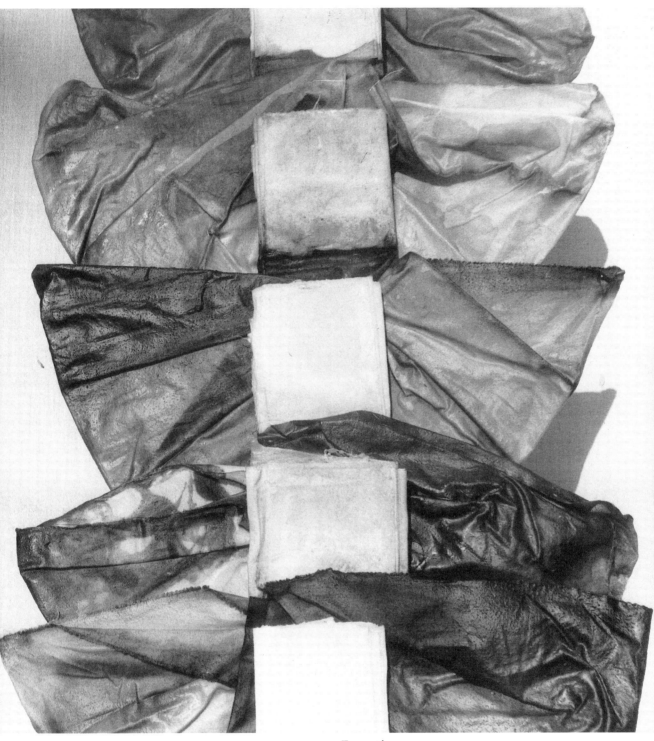

95 Formation
*Sculpture detail. Cotton, naphthol-dyed with
repeated dips in wax until solid, 1984.*

resilient the wax, the whiter the ground. The thinner wax will submit to the dye penetration and create shades and variations to the ground colour.

- Take the above a step further; remove the wax and rework from light to dark. With a predetermined, positive image, the artist can impose sequences of overlays without changing the graphic form. Substantial changes can occur, however, in the white areas to build up an integrated design. The advantage of this approach is to enable the artist to liberate the intermediary processes within an established structure.

96 Accidents will happen! A drop of wax mistakenly placed can be removed by first scraping the bulk of the wax off with a knife, then, after placing absorbent paper behind the spot and damping it, apply the tip of a hot iron until it dissolves. Take care not to scorch the cloth. When it is dry, check to see if you need to repeat the process. Alternatively, accept it as fate and make the best of it.

97 Re-waxing on a previously discharged and wax-free cloth.

By using a variety of colours, part dipping, spraying and painting, the artist can amass an amazing spectrum of colour between waxings. Remove the wax and rewax to capture the fusion of colour under strict forms. Dye black to dramatize the effect.

To reverse the negative concept of the conventional batik, dye the cloth black, wax the design and discharge the exposed colour. The bleached-out background then offers the opportunity to work from light to dark whilst retaining the black form under the wax.

PAINTING ON SILK USING GUTTA RESIST TECHNIQUES

This method was introduced into France in the early 1920s by Russian immigrants who painted silks by hand. The colours used are based on the original aniline synthetic dyes, although a number of French dyes are now produced without aniline and are consequently non-toxic.

The dyes are popular because they are liquid, economical and easily applied with a brush as well as having a lustre and transparency on silk that is very impressive.

The range is flexible, varying from pale tints through vibrant hues to dark, rich shades.

Procedure

(1) Prepare the design on silk and set onto the frame with pins.

(2) The gutta resist is applied either with a cone or pipette. The gutta is a fluid latex, thinned with a solvent or water to the correct consistency for use. An effective resist would penetrate the silk to create a waterproof barrier that dyes cannot penetrate. The gutta should be thinned just before use.

98 Silk scarf detail by Tacy Long. Black gutta resist, 55 × 55cm, 1987

If left it will evaporate and become too sticky to penetrate.

Test the gutta carefully. The correct consistency is that of liquid honey; it should not take more than ten minutes to dry in the silk mesh. Plastic pipettes are the simplest applicators to use; pierce the spout with a fine needle and, cap it with a barrel pen (these come in a range of sizes).

A cone is fashioned from glassine paper or tracing paper and is favoured by the professional artist as it is more flexible and produces a refined line. To make a cone take a piece of paper 15 × 25cm (6 × 10in.). Roll it so that the tip comes in the centre of the longest side and place masking tape at the seam. Half fill the cone with gutta and press down to the tip with the fingers. Seal and make it air-tight. The tip can be cut open slightly to allow a wider flow.

Hold the top of the applicator and apply steady pressure by hand to achieve a consistent line on the silk design. To avoid drips or blobs clean excess gutta from the spout before each new application. Use a bevel-edged ruler to draw straight lines. Mistakes can be removed by rubbing the gutta with a pad of white spirit and an absorbent cotton pad on the reverse side.

(3) Having checked the gutta to forestall any leaks, you may now paint on the dye. Begin by filling the centre areas to enable the colour to spread to the barrier on its own accord. Work quickly, but don't overfill with colour. For graduated effects, dry the base colour before applying the second. Stains in dye painting can be softened by applying small amounts of pure alcohol on cotton buds. Use brushes appropriate to the size of the area to be covered. Halo effects are caused by a slow or over-brushing technique.

Additional special effects can be created by sprinkling dry crystal or cooking salt on a wet dye surface. It absorbs both the water and alcohol leaving spectacular swirling eruptions on the surface design. Remove the salt when dry. Alternatively, apply a mixture of water and alcohol to discharge the colour pigment.

(4) To fix colour by steaming roll the silk pieces in a porous paper such as wrapping or lining paper. Don't overlap or crease the silk. If, on steaming, the gutta is not absorbed, soak the silk in white spirit. The superior vibrancy of the steam-fixed dyes over the recommended alternatives makes the effort worth while.

Complete instructions on steam fixation are at the end of chapter 4.

Range of suitable French dyes for silk and wool

These companies also produce dilutants and gutta: Dupont; Kniazeff; Princecolor and Sennelier Super Tinfix.

seven

A GALLERY
OF BATIK ARTISTS

FRITZ DONART
Austria

99 Images of wood and water by Fritz Donart
Cotton, 54 × 95cm, 1984

Fritz Donart travelled to Java in 1972 and studied under Astuti, Hadji and the late Bambang Oetoro and Kuswadji. Exhibited regularly in Europe.

There is the wisdom of the five elements, the basic knowledge of eastern healing, which corresponds to my practice of Tai Chi and

batik: the wax I use, I get from animals and trees (*wood*). Mother *earth* gives the paraffin with those typical cracks within the fabric, like dried clay of a river. The *fire* melts these elements together and I am able to use this liquid in the canting (*metal*). The canting in my hand follows my thoughts. Cold *water* is used to

bring colours and boiling water frees the batik from the covered wax. With these elements I feel like an alchemist, trying to catch the microcosmic visions within the microcosmic realization of texile art.

TONY DYER
Australia

Tony Dyer is a senior lecturer at the Melbourne College of Advanced Education and has had 12 major exhibitions since 1970. His work has been represented in many public collections in Australia including the Art Gallery of Western Australia. He won the Craftsperson of 1985 award.

Like most craftspeople using the batik process I was self-taught. The influence of my formal studies on a printed textile design course greatly influenced my early work in the 1960s. Drawings made of surroundings and places visited became stronger focal points linked with a greater understanding of dyes, waxes and the nature of silk. The graphic nature of the medium – drawn lines and painted/dipped/sprayed etc. colour – lent itself to the images

100 Altar piece by Tony Dyer
Silk, naphthol and reactive-dyed, 1.5 × 5.3m, 1983/4, (commissioned by Yarra Valley Grammar School, Ringwood, Victoria, Australia).

and became a blend of stylized patterned forms. Gradually these blended with the silk surface and created a collage form, often sandwiched between acrylic sheets, but occasionally combined with stitch, wood and cane which also has been waxed and dyed. Recent work comprises a more even, demanding sculptural approach with more subtle uses of colour and soft surface texture.

SHIGEKI FUKUMOTO
Japan

Shigeki Fukumoto obtained a Master of Fine Arts degree at Kyoto University and in 1970 he

101 Topological space-B by Shigeki Fukumoto
Cotton, 176 × 88cm, 1981.

established a kimono dyeing studio. He is now a research writer on tribal arts and a lecturer in wax resist dyeing at Huraku Textile Academy, Kyoto.

Fukumoto chose the roketsu-zome technique after studying painting for six years because 'the skill is free, delicate and unrestricted expressing directly the aesthetic sense and conceptions of the artist, and one which can create a highly individual personal style'.

The processes are made up of many stages; preparing and stretching the cloth on fine bamboo rods, waxing either directly with a brush or scattering wax with a stencil as a restraining form. (The Japanese word for this is *hubuki* meaning snowstorm.) Dye is brushed over the resist in graduated and subtle shadings. Innumerable repeats of these processes build up the richness of design. The wax is removed by washing in hot petrol. My source for *Blue N Dimension* (*see* colour section) was the tra-

ditional *byobu* screen, which is ingenious; it is light, easy to display and has various uses. 'The flat screen is two-dimensional, folded it becomes three. I want to create a fourth dimension.'

HENK MAK
Holland

Henk Mak has exhibited regularly in Holland and works within the state support scheme for artists. He was trained in Java in 1972. He has adopted a non-decorative, realistic style, mainly figurative work.

> My batik work liberated itself from the tradition and now I'm employing crack-wax, special dye processes and brush painting. Getting away from the colours, sobering up and discovering an unknown potential!

*102 **Nude** by Henk Mak*
Cotton, 90 × 135cm, 1981.

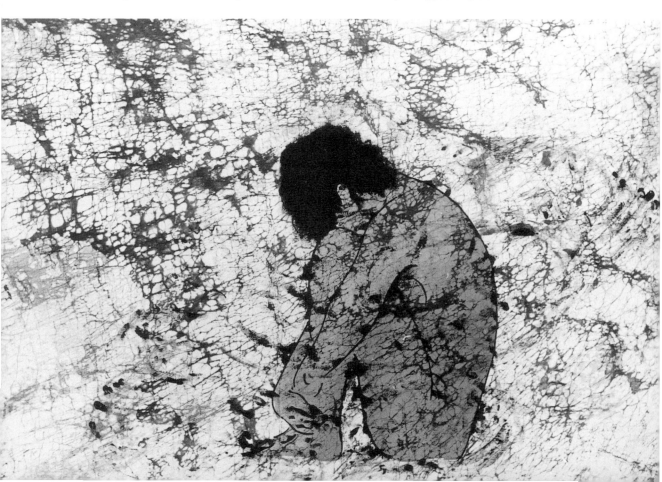

MIEP SPÉE
Holland

103 Check and fold by Miep Spée
Cotton, naphthol-dyed, 80 × 100cm, 1979.

Miep Spée graduated in 1965 from the Academy of Industrial Design, Eindhaven. She has been a part-time teacher in textile art since 1975.

By using the batik technique I combine my affinity for paint colour and textile material. Originally I made use of this technique in a more 'painterly' way and worked on a very smooth surface; the textile only had a surface function. In the mid-seventies I turned my attention more and more to the possibilities of the material itself, giving the material an independent role. By concentrating on its pliability and suppleness, the material became a means of expression and subject as well.

Turning to a less formal concept of work I used another character aspect of the material; its structure. With this I attach an independent function to the textile material which combines real and illusionary pleats and folds in the play with checks and stripes.

NORMA STARSZAKOWNA
Britain

Norma Starszakowna graduated in 1966 in printed textiles and printmaking from Duncan of

104 Shade/shadow by Norma Starszakowna
Silk, basic dyes, 41 × 42cm, 1982.

Jordanstone College of Art, Dundee. She then established her own studio. Currently she is Head of Textiles at Duncan of Jordanstone. She exhibited regularly and the awards she has won include the 1983 Saltine Society, Art in Architecture. Her work is included in collections at the Scottish Arts Council, the Scottish Crafts Council, IBM, and Leeds City Art Gallery.

I was drawn to batik by the immediacy of the medium and the translucency of the dyes – these seem to be a perfect vehicle for expressing certain inherent qualities of cloth; its strength and fragility, perhaps its omnipresence. Most earlier work depicts folded and layered cloth, sometimes with a burned edge, often image layered upon image. Recent work becomes three-dimensional: bowls in treated/stiffened silk, sometimes combined with acetate film. Concepts evolved around a consideration of shade/shadow, its connotations and associations. This involves prisms; shaded lights; sunglasses (regimes – people who wear them to hide their eyes) light of the nations; lampshades (fragments, tattooed skin); the shadow cast by such things, shades themselves.

Her technique is as follows:
(1) First she waxes the broken lines and grid.
(2) She dips the silk in pale grey dye and waxes the square behind grid.

105 Bisalam by Amri Yahya
Cotton, naphthol and indigosol dyes, 80 × 100cm, 1972.

(3) She shades deeper grey dye shaded onto wet silk using cotton wool. She then waxes the second square behind the grid, as well as four smaller fragments on broken lines.

(4) The silk is dipped in very pale orange to give a beige colour. The third square behind the grid is waxed.

(5) Various coloured dyes are shaded onto some of the smaller fragments inside the grid, using cotton wool on wet silk. These are then waxed.

(6) The silk is dipped in pale pink. The figure at top is then partially waxed and deeper tones of dye washed up to the waxed edge. This is done repeatedly, using a fine canting on areas such as folds, elbow, nose, fingers, etc., until the required amount of detail is achieved and the figure is completely waxed including the adjacent lines.

(7) The silk is dipped in deeper orange; wax is brushed over and beyond the figures, giving a smooth arc, but leaving free the brush stroke end.

(8) She then dips the silk into black dye.

AMRI YAHYA
Indonesia

Amri Yahya is a leading innovative batik artist in Indonesia. He graduated from the Academy of Fine Arts, Yogykarta, in 1961 and is currently a lecturer at the Islamic University. He has founded many cultural enterprises including the White Studio, a young artists' organization, in 1970 and he established his own gallery in 1972. Amongst other artistic activities he was the executor of the First National Exhibitions and Head of the Indonesian Artists' Conference. He has travelled widely and has had exhibitions in the Arab States, America and Europe. His works is included in many eminent collections, including those of the Director General of Unesco, King Saudi, and the National Gallery of Kuwait.

I choose batik as the medium of art expression because of its inherent origin in the Indonesian culture, generation to generation.

Batik is close to the social daily life. It has a high and everlasting value in history and culture in our society. As a painter I wanted to find something new, batik painting was considered a new medium and I love it and will paint with it forever. It is a supreme medium in painting. I wish to unify earth through art!

106 Brushing on indigosol developing solution.

142

107 4 square
Silk, 40 × 40cm each,
1988.

'My work attempts
to explore the
tensions between the
state and the
individual – the
battle between the
overall public
systems of
uniformity and
subjugation and the
flourishing of the
inner spirit.
Uncertain times
nurture absolutes,
and strictures are
imposed on
individual identity.
I try to transcend
this state of
absolutes by
creating a flux of
images and layers
that return us to the
diverse, personal
world of the self.'

Noel Dyrenforth,
1988

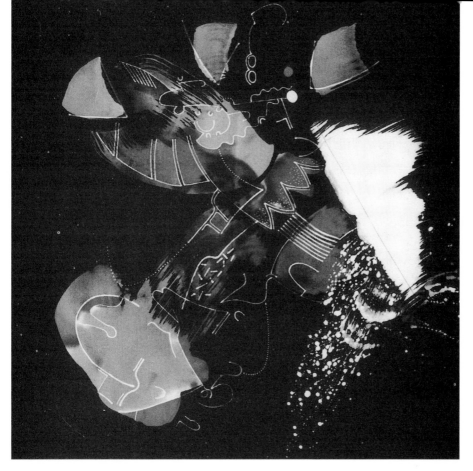

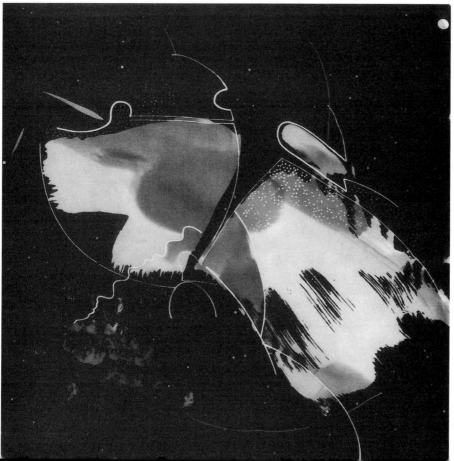

CONVERSION TABLES OF WEIGHTS AND MEASURES

TEMPERATURE CONVERSION TABLE

Volume	Metric equivalent
$\frac{1}{4}$ teaspoon	1ml
1 teaspoon	5ml
1 tablespoon	15ml
1 fluid ounce	30ml
$\frac{1}{2}$ cup	120ml
1 pint	480ml
1 quart	950ml (nearly 1 litre)
1 gallon	3.8ol.

Weight	Metric equivalent
1 ounce	28g.
4 ounces	113g.
8 ounces	227g.
16 ounces (1 pound)	454g.
2.2 pounds	1kg.
1 teaspoon	approximately 3g.

All substances, dyestuffs and chemicals have different weight values and cannot be equated by volume.

Length	Metric equivalent
1 inch	2.54cm
1 foot	0.305m
1 yard	0.91m
1 mile	1.61km

Temperature conversion table

$32°F = 0°C$ (freezing point of water)
$212°F = 100°C$ (boiling point of water)
$132°F = 56°C$ (melting point of paraffin)
$136°F = 58°C$ (melting point of beeswax)
$166°F = 75°C$ (melting point of microcrystalline)

GLOSSARY

Acid dye   A chemical which is mainly sodium salts of organic acids assisted by salt. It is an acid or acid-producing compound in the dyebath, which has an affinity with silk and wool.

Affinity   Special chemical attraction of a dye to unify with a fabric.

Aniline dyes   The first synthetic dyes made with aniline as the basis. Aniline unites with acid to form colour salts.

Assistant   Chemical dye recipe that aids the bond between dye and fibre.

Azoic dyes   These dyes form colour on the fibre, usually cotton, by impregnating with naphthol and then coupling with a diazo salt bath. The dyes are very fast to boil and light and are used extensively in Javanese batiks today.

Beeswax   The malleable quality of beeswax insures a flexible and substantial resist which corrodes less than synthetic resists when chemicals are added.

Bleach   Process of discharging colour from fibres by chemical means.

Bleeding   Loss of dye colour, usually in the washing.

Calgon   Water softening agent.

Canting (*pronounced chănting and originally spelt, tjanting*)   Tool for applying wax with which hand-drawn tulis batik is made.

Cap (*pronounced chăp and originally spelt, tjap*)   Copper block stamp to apply wax to cloth.

Caustic soda   Sodium hydroxide is the effective agent for mercerizing cotton. It is used in naphthol as an alkali.

Cellulose   The basic material of all vegetable fibres, cotton, flax and new Viscose Rayon.

Chemical water (Calgon)   Chemically known as sodium hexametaphosphate, it acts as a sequestering agent, neutralizing any interference in water to the normal reaction of dyes.

Colour   Depends on three measurable qualities: hue; degree of lightness or darkness; and intensity.

Cone drawing (tsutsugaki)   Freehand style application of resist paste, using a mulberry paper brass-tipped cone.

Crocking   Unfixed dye which rubs off cloth surface.

Dip   Immersion of cloth into dye bath.

Direct application   Includes painting on, spraying, blocking dyes, pigments or resists onto the surface of the cloth.

Direct dyes   A cotton dye simple to apply with the addition of salt. Poor fastness, but improves with after-treatment.

Discharge   Removal of colour, also called bleaching or stripping.

Dodot   Batik cloth made by joining two kains together (2×4m) used for ceremonial occasions.

Dressing   A mixture applied to give a finish to the cloth surface. Best removed before dyeing.

Dry cleaning   Cleaning fabric by treating with an organic solvent.

Dyebath   Solution of dyestuff, assistants and water in which the cloth is immersed.

Exhaust   The degree by which the cloth takes up the full colour potential of the dyebath.

Fastness   The cloth's colour-resistance, particularly to light and washing.

Fibre-reactive dyes   Cold water dye which reacts to alkaline solution to form a bond between the dye molecule and the fibre. It is intermixable, reliable, fast and simple to use on cotton and silk.

Fixing   The process of making the colour permanent to ensure fastness.

Garuda   Mythical bird of Indonesia, symbol of heaven.

Glauber's salt   Sodium sulphide, which encourages level dyeing.

Gringsing   A fish-scale motif which patterns the background of Indonesian batiks.

Gutta   Gutta-percha is a colourless rubber latex used as a resist. It is applied to the material with either a plastic pipette or cone.

Hera   Spatula used for applying resist paste through a stencil.

Hikizome brushes   A ground colour brush with wide handle and deer hair bristles, which absorbs large amounts of dye.

Ikat   Wrapping yarns to a pattern resist, dyed and woven.

Iket kapala   Batik headcloth.

Indigo   Made from the leaves of the plant, *Indigofera*, this dye is distributed widely throughout the tropical areas of the world. Historically indigo is the oldest and most important of dyestuffs. Synthetic indigo came onto the market in 1897, and was soon cheaper and more convenient to use than the natural product.

Lissapol   Detergent and wetting agent.

Ludigol   Chemical that prevents reduction.

Kain panjang   Long cloth, approximately two to three metres (6.5–10ft) long, densely decorated with batik designs and with border at one end.

Katazome   Paste-resist stencil dyeing.

Kemben   A narrow batik cloth used around the upper body to fasten a sarong.

Kepala   The perpendicular band that contrasts with the main design area of the sarong.

Kraton   Javanese palace.

Levelling agent   An assistant that promotes the level distribution of colour on the cloth.

Liquor ratio   The relation of the water in a dyebath to the weight of the cloth.

Lye   Caustic soda (sodium hydroxide) solution.

Mercerizing   Treatment of cellulose cloth with concentrated caustic soda to improve lustre and strengthen the fibres' affinity with the dye.

Microcrystalline wax   Synthetic, substance derived from petroleum. It is used as a substitute for beeswax.

Migration   Movement of dye from one part of the cloth to another.

Monopol brilliant oil   Stabilizer and softener for naphtol dyebaths.

Mordant   Chemical that combines with the dye molecule in the cloth to form an insoluble compound.

Naphthol dyes   *See* Azoic dyes.

Nori   Rice paste resist.

Overdyeing   Placing one colour dye over another.

Oxidation   Exposure of the dyed cloth to air; in vat dyeing this converts the colour back into its insoluble form to bond it to the fibre.

Pagi-sore   A batik sarong which can be adjusted to be worn as morning or evening wear. Each half has a separate design.

Paraffin wax   Soft, translucent wax derived from petroleum. It is brittle and less resistant than microcrystalline wax. Marbling effects are created by using a greater percentage of paraffin in the recipe.

Parang   A diagonal 'broken-knife' batik motif on a sarong, at one time worn exclusively by the nobility in Java.

Pigment   Powder forms, mixed with a resin-bound, are coated onto the fabric, giving an opacity and slight stiffening to the texture.

Plangi   Technique of resist tying and dyeing cloth.

Prepared for printing   Fabric that has been scoured, degummed and bleached.

Protein fibre   Animal material for making wool and silk.

Rayon   Man-made fibre made from cellulose. Viscose Rayon dyes as well as cotton.

Resist salt L   A mild oxidizing agent that prevents the dye from decomposing during fixation and achieves a high colour yield.

Roketsu-zome   Japanese batik method.

Salt   Sodium chloride used as an assistant in reactive and direct dyes.

Sarong   Javanese or Malay waistcloth originally from India.

Scouring   Removing impurities from fabric by washing in soap or detergent in preparation for dyeing.

Shade   To add a small quantity of dye to increase colour shade.

Shrinkage   Contraction of cloth from heat or moisture processes.

Sizing   Application of starch or coating agent to enhance finish on cloth.

Slendang   Long, narrow cloth used by Javanese women.

Soda ash   Mild alkali, known as sodium carbonate (a form of washing soda) causes procion M dyes to react in fibre.

Sodium alginate (manutex)   A gum extract from seaweed, used as a thickening agent.

Sodium bi-carbonate (baking powder)   A mild alkaline used in reactive dyeing for painting on colour.

Sodium bisulphite   A quick, inexpensive chemical for discharge dyeing. It contains chlorine.

Sodium hydrosulphite   A less powerful discharge agent than chlorine bleach.

Soga   Rich brown dye derived mainly from the bark of a tree.

Steaming   Moist heat process for fixing dye colour.

Stock solution   Prepared chemical or dye solution to a specific ratio.

Synthetic dyes   The early man-made dyes made from the aniline contained in coal tar were not particularly successful. It was not until 1868 with the discovery of synthetic alizarin that they replaced the natural product commercially.

Thickener   A gel-like substance used to increase the consistency in painting on dye.

Tulis   The hand-drawn batik method.

Tumpal   A band designed with triangles that run down the ends of a batik sarong.

Union dye   A dye mixture suited to two or more blended fibres.

Urea   A mild alkali synthesized from natural gas, used as a moisture-retaining agent.

Vat dyes   These dyes are insoluble in water and must be dissolved chemically before being applied to fabric. Colour develops by exposure to heat and light or an oxidizing agent. Suitable for cotton and silk.

Vinegar   Contains acetic acid and is used in dyeing silk and wool.

Washing off   To wash off surplus dye or ingredients out of cloth which will interfere with further dyeing of the cloth or the natural finished texture.

Whetting out   To assure more even and level colour the cloth is dampened before dyeing.

Yuzen   A particular fine dye painting style, contained by resist-paste outlines.

LIST OF BATIK SUPPLIERS, ORGANIZATIONS, PERIODICALS, MUSEUMS, AND GALLERIES

United Kingdom

Suppliers

Atlantis Art
E2 Warehouse
New Crane Wharf
Garner Street
London E1
(Gutta, Tinfix, silk, Japanese brushes, steamers and excellent range of papers) (Mail order)

Candle Makers Suppliers
28 Blythe Road
London W14
(Procion, kniazeff, Deka dyes, beeswax and synthetic waxes, cantings, videos, books and helpful advice) (Mail order)

Durham Chemical Distributors Ltd
55–57 Glengall Road
London SE15
(Procion, Kenactive, acid and direct dyes, chemicals)

Dylon International Ltd
139–151 Sydneham Road
London
(Fibre-reactive and multi-purpose dyes)

Noel Dyrenforth
11 Shepherds Hill
London N6
(Procion, Javanese cantings, teaching courses)

ICI (Imperial Chemical Industries Ltd)
Blackley
Manchester
(Procion, Brenthol, Soledan dyestuffs' manufacturer)

Macculloch & Wallis Ltd
25 Dering Street
London W1
(Ranges of cotton and silk)

Pongees Ltd
184–6 Old Street
London EC1
(Wide range of silks, crêpe satin, crêpe de chine, habotai, spun, twill, etc.)

Poth Hike & Co Ltd
37 High Street
Stratford
London E15
(Ranges of waxes including micro, paraffin and beeswax)

Printex Fabrics Ltd
P.O. Box 830
35 Westgate
Huddersfield
Yorks
(Fine cotton range, including Egyptian and mercerized)

George Weil & Sons Ltd
63–65 Riding Horse Street
London W1
(Procion, Tinfix, Deka dyes, wax, gutta, cantings, silk and cotton) (Mail order)

Whaleys (Bradford) Ltd
Harris Court
Great Horton
Bradford
W. Yorkshire
(Silk, cotton, calico, jute, linen and wool)

Organizations

Contemporary Applied Arts
43 Earlham Street
London WC2

Crafts Council
12 Waterloo Place
London SW1
(Gallery and information centre. Slide index of
selected craftspeople in the UK. Education ser-
vices and publications)

Periodicals

Crafts
8 Waterloo Place
London SW1
(Bi-monthly published by the Crafts Council)

Museums and Galleries

The British Museum
Great Russell Street
London WC1

Joss Graham Textile Gallery
10 Eccleston Street
London SW1

Museum of Mankind
(British Museum, Dept of Ethnography)
6 Burlington Gardens
London W1
(The Charles Beving collection of batiks is
superb)

Victoria & Albert Museum
South Kensington
London SW7

United States of America

Suppliers

Aiko's Art Materials Import
714 North Wabash Avenue
Chicago
Illinois 60611
(Katazome supplies, brushes, dyes)

Aljo Manufacturing Co Ltd
116 Prince Street
New York, NY 10012
(Chemical and dyes: acid, basic, direct, reactive,
naphthol and vat)

Cerulean Blue Ltd
P.O. Box 21168
119 Blanchard Street
Seattle WA 98111
(The best stocked and most professionally in-
formed textile art suppliers: Procion, Deka, Ciba
vat and acid dyes, Japanese brushes for dye
painting and waxing, Katazome supplies, fine
cottons and silks, comprehensive list of books. A
gallery also attached.) (Mail order)

Colour Craft Ltd
P.O. Box 936 Avon
CT 06001

Dharma Trading Company
P.O. Box 916
San Rafael CA 94902
(Dyes, fabrics and chemicals)

Fabdec
3553 Old Post Road
San Angelo
TX 76901
(Procion, chemical, fabrics)

Fibrec
1154 Howard Street
P.O. Box 985
San Francisco
CA 94103

Hoechst Corp
129 Quidnick Street
Coventry
RI O 2816

ICI United States Inc
Dyes and Textiles Chemical Division
Concord Pike and Murphy Rd
Wilmington, DE 19897

Ivy Crafts Imports
5410 Annapolis Road
Blandensburg
Maryland 20710
(Sennelier, Tintix and gutta)

Organizations

American Crafts Council
Research and Education Dept.
401 Park Avenue
New York 10016

Embassy of Indonesia
Information Division
Chancery
2020 Massachusetts Avenue NW
Washington, DC 20036

Surface Design Association Inc
Art Department
North Texas State University
P.O. Box 5098
Denton
Texas 76203
(Organizes conferences, workshops, technical and news magazine. Slide kits on contemporary international batik artists. Publishes Surface Design Journal *quarterly)*

Periodicals

American Crafts
401 Park Avenue South
New York 10016

Fiberarts
Lark Communication
50 College Street
Asheville
North Carolina 28801

Surface Design Journal
311 East Washington Street
Fayetteville, NN 37334

Museums and Galleries

Louise Allrich Gallery (Textile Art)
251 Post Street
San Francisco, CA 94108

American Craft Museum
45 West 45 Street
New York, NY 10036

Textile Museum
Washington, DC

Textile Study Center
University of Washington
Seattle

Australia

Suppliers

Batik Oetoro
P.O. Box 324
Coogee
NSW 2034
(Fibre reactives, naphthol, indigosol, vat dyes, acid dyes, chemicals, waxes, silk, cotton, imports of Javanese cotton, cantings and stoves. Excellent information sheets on dyeing and waxing recipes) (Mail order)

Marcus Arts
372 Drummond Street
Charlton, Victoria 3056
(Naphthol, Procion, acid dyes, waxes, tools and fabric)

Periodicals

Craft Arts
PO Box 363
Neutral Bay Junction
NSW 2089

Craft Australia
100 George Street
The Rocks
Sydney
2000

Organizations

The Batik Association of Australia
P.O. Box 85
Coogee
NSW 2034
(Regular newsletter specializing in technical information, exhibitions and events)

Crafts Council of Australia
100 George Street
The Rocks
Sydney 2000
(Represents craftspeople, arranges exhibitions and produces slides, books and periodicals)

Fibre Forum
The Australian Forum for Textile Arts
P.O. Box 77
University of Queensland
Brisbane

Museums and Galleries

National Museum of Victoria
180 St Kilda Road
Melbourne 3004

Art Gallery of Western Australia
Perth

China

Museums

Guizhou Batik Art Academy
270 Waihuan Dong Rd
Guiyang
Guizhou

France

Suppliers

H. Dupont
11 Rue du Faubourg St Denis
75010
Paris
(Manufacturer of batik, silk/wool painting dyes and gutta)

Kniazeff
Ateliers Créatiff
18 Rue de Garet
69001 Lyons
(Silk/wool painting dyes)

R. Leprince SA
19 Rue de Clery
75002 Paris
(Silk/wool painting dyes)

Sennelier
Rue de Moulin á Cailloux
Orley, Sénia
408–945671 Rungis Cedex
(Manufacturer of Tinfix silk/wool dyes)

Periodicals

Textile Art
3 Rue Felix-Faure
73015 Paris

Germany

Suppliers

Deka-Textilfarben
D-8025 Munchen
(Manufacturer of Deka L and Deka silk dyes)

Galerie Smend
Mainzer Strasse 31, 37
PO 250450
D-5000
Cologne
(Extensive range of batik materials. Catalogue available. Naphthol, re-active, Princecolour, silk dyes, gutta, waxes, Javanese cantings, fabrics, books and periodicals.) (Excellent, comprehensive mail order catalogue and service)

Hoechst AG
D-6230
Frankfurt 80
(Manufacturer of Anthrasol, Naphthol-AS, Ramazol)

Periodicals

Kunst und Handwerk
Auf' Tetelberg 7
Postfach 8120
D-4000
Dusseldorf 1

Textilforum
Friedenstr 1
Postfach 5944
D-3000
Hanover 1

Textilkunst
Verlag M & H Schaper
Grazerstrasse 20
Postfach 810669
D-3000
Hanover 81

Museums

Deutsches Textilmuseum
Andreasmarkt 8
4150 Krefeld
12-Linn

Gallerie Smend
Mainzer Strasse 31, 37
PO 250450
D-5000
Cologne
(Contemporary and traditional batik collection, study and library area. Comprehensive programmes of batik activities, courses, tours to Java, supervised by Rudolf Smend)

Holland

Suppliers

Luvotex
Post. 853.
2300 AW
Leiden
(Dyes, wax, traditional cantings, silk and cotton)

Museums

Koninklijk Institute Voor de Tropen
Mauritskade 63
Amsterdam

Stedelijk Museum
Paulus Potterstraat 13
Amsterdam

India

Organizations

Batik Art Research and Training Institute
50 Silwat wari
Udaipur
India

Indonesia

Suppliers

Sawojajar
Jl Panerbahan 1
Yogjakarta. Java.
(Cantings, resin, wax; primissima, prima, biro and merah qualities of cotton. Naphthol and indigosol dyes)

Organizations

Batik Research Centre
Jl. Kusumanegara 2
Yogyakarta

Galleries

Amri Yahya Gallery
Gampigan 67
Yogyakarta

Kuswadji Gallery
Jl. Alun Alun Utara Pojok Barat Daya
Yogyakarta

Tulus Warsito Gallery
Jl. Tirtodipuran 19A
Yogyakarta 55143
(Also run batik courses)

Japan

Suppliers

Tanaka Nao Dyes Supplies
Ogawa
Sanjodori
Chuo-Ku
Kyoto 604
and
3-9-8 Shibuya
Shibuya-Ku
Tokyo 150
(Dyes, chemicals, fabric, roketsu-zome and katazome and books) (Mail order)

Organizations

Japan Craft Design Association
21-13 Sendagaya-1
Shibuya-Ku
Tokyo 151

Juraku International Textile Centre
Karasuma-dori
Kuramaguchi-Sagaru
Kamigyo-Ku
Kyoto 602
(For research into traditional and contemporary textiles, international exchange and promotion of textile art)

Periodicals

Textile Arts Magazine
Shikosha Publishing Co Ltd
Kyoto

Senshoku
Senshoku To Seikatsu-Sha Publishers
Nishiiru Karasumaru
Matsubaradoori, Shimokyo-ku
Kyoto

Switzerland

Museum

Museum fur Volkerkunde
Basel

BIBLIOGRAPHY

DJOEMENA, Nian, *Batik, its Mystery and Meaning*, Djambatan, Jakarta, 1986.

DYRENFORTH, Noel (with John Houston), *Batik with Noel Dyrenforth*, Orbis Publishing Co. Ltd, London, 1975.
Dutch Text: Uitgeverij Kosmos bv Amsterdam, 1977.

ELLIOTT, Inger McCabe, *Batik Fabled Cloth of Java*, Clarkson N. Potter Inc., New York, 1984.

FLOWER, Lynda, *Ideas and Techniques for Fabric Design*, Longman, London, 1986.

GITTINGER, Mattiebelle, *Indonesian Textiles*, Textile Museum, Washington, DC, 1980.

GITTINGER, Mattiebelle, *Splendid Symbols, Textiles & Traditions in Indonesia*, Eastern Press, New Haven, 1979.

HAAKE, Annegret, *Javanische Batik, Methode-Symbolik-Geschichte*, Verlag M. and H. Schaper, Hanover, 1984.

HOLT, Claire, *Art in Indonesia: Continuity & Change*, Cornell University Press, New York, 1967.

HUNTER, I, *Dyeing with Naphthol Dyes*, Batik Oetoro, Sydney, 1977.

HUNTER, I, *Dyeing with Fibre Reactive Dyes*, Batik Oetoro, Sydney, 1977.

ICI DYESTUFFS DIVISION, *Introduction to Textile Printing*, Butterworth & Co., London, 1964.

LARSEN, Jack Lenor, *The Dyer's Art*, Van Norstrand Reinhold, New York, 1976.

LOEBER, J.A., *Das Batiken Eine Blute, Indonesian Kunstlelebens*, Gerhard Stelling Verlag, Germany, 1925.

MAXWELL, John & Robyn, *Textiles of Indonesia*, Gardner Printing & Publishing, Melbourne, 1976.

MIJER, P., *Batiks and How To Make Them*, Dodd Mead & Co., New York, 1925.

MEILACH, Dona, *Contemporary Batik & Tie Dye*, Allen & Unwin, London, 1973.

MONZIE, A. de, *Les Batiks De Madame Pangon*, Editions D'Art Charles Moreau, Paris, 1925.

NAKANO, Eisha (with B. Stephan), *Japanese Stencil Dyeing*, Weatherhill Inc., New York & Tokyo, 1982.

NEÁ, Sara, *Batik*, Van Norstrand Reinhold, 1970.

PICTON, John & MACK, J., *African Textiles*, British Museum, London, 1979.

PROCTOR, Richard & LEW, Jennifer, *Surface design for fabric*, University of Washington Press, Seattle & London, 1984.

RAFFLES, Thomas Stamford, *The History of Java*, (Reprint of 1817 edition), Oxford University Press, Kaula Lumpur, Malaysia, 1982.

ROBINSON, Stuart, *The History of Dyed Textiles*, Studio Vista Ltd, London, 1969.

STEINMANN, Dr Alfred *Batik, a Survey of Batik Design*, F. Lewis Publishers, UK, 1958.

STEINMANN, Dr Alfred, *Batiks*, CIBA Review No. 58, Basel, Switzerland, 1947.

SOETOPO, S., *Batik*, P.T. Indira Publishers, Jakarta, Indonesia, 1983.

SPÉE, Miep, *Traditional & Modern Batiks*, Kangaroo Press, Australia, 1977.

STOREY, Joyce, *Dyes and Fabrics*, Thames & Hudson Ltd, London, 1978.

SUTTON, Anne, *British Craft Textiles*, William Collins, London, 1985.

THOMAS, Michel, *Textile Art*, Weidenfeld & Nicholson, London, 1985.

URSIN, A. & KILCHENMANN, *Batik, Harmonie mit Wachs und Farbe*, Paul Haupt, Berne, Switzerland, 1979.

VICTORIA & ALBERT MUSEUM, *Batiks*, HMSO, London, 1969.

WARMING, Wanda & GAWORSKI, Michael, *The World of Indonesian Textiles*, Kadansha International Ltd, 1981.

INDEX

Acetic acid 66, 72, 111
Acid dyes 72
Africa 3
Ajunta caves 4
Alkali 64–5
Anglo 27
Azoic dyes 67

Bambara tribe 17
Basic dyes 72
Beeswax 27, 49–51
Bingata 21
Biron 30
Bleaching 72, 131
Block printing 59
Boiling out wax 30, 33, 111
Brentamine fast black K-salt 65
Brushes 56–59, 93, 101, 115

Calgon 65–6
Canting
  brush 27
  cleaning 55–6, 85
  electric 52
  glass 15
  use 25, 27, 53–55, 60, 92, 100
Cap 27
  making 32–3
  printing 33–5
Casava paste 17
Caustic soda 68, 106
Chemicals 65, 68
Chemical water 66
Chinese influence 11, 18, 30
Cirebon 28, 37
Cleaning solvents 98
Complementary colours 61

Cones 20, 131
Cotton 25, 46

Damar gum 51
Deka dye 71
Design 61
Diazo colour salt 68
Direct dye application 115
  fixation 67
  french dyes 131–2
  indigosol 71
  naphthol 69–70
  procion 66, 80
Dodot 40
Donart, Fritz 133
Dye history 63
Dye theory 63
Dyeing procedures
  chemicals 65, 68
  direct or Application dyes 71
  dye bath 82–3
  fast K salt 65–7
  fibre reactive dyes 64, 87–92
  fixation 67, 74, 132
  indigo dyeing 27–8
  naphthol or azoic dyes
    67–70, 102–110
  natural dyes 28
  percentage-dye solution 64
  ratio-dye bath 63
  soga 28–9
  synthetic dyes 63
  thickener 66
Dyer, Tony 134

Easter eggs 23
Edo period 23

Egypt 13
Etching 121–2
Exploration 59
Fast K salt 65
Fastness 64, 66–7
Fibre-reactive dyes 64–6
Finishing 74
Fixation 74
Frame 78
French silk dyes 132
Fukumoto, Shigeki 134

Glauber's salt 72
Gutta 132

Haarlem school of batik 15
Heating wax 53
Holland 13–15
Hue 61
Hydrochloric acid 72

Imitation batik 15
Immersion dyeing method 82–3,
  87–92
India 19
Indigo 27–8
Indigosol 71
Ironing out 97

Japan 19–23
Java 13
Javanese,
  dancers 36
  dress 40
  patterns 37–40

Kain 41
Katazome 19
Kent, Irene 125
Kepala 41
Klowong wax 29–30

Leather 126
Lebeau, Chris 14
Linen 46
Lissapol 65
Long, Tacy 130

Madura 29
Manchester wax prints 22–3
Metapex 98
Miao tribe 18
Microcrystalline wax 27, 49
Monochrome batik 28–9
Mordant 27
Multicoloured brush dyeing 80

Naphthol dyes 67–70
    colour mixing 70
    recipe 68
    procedure 68–70, 102–10
Nara screens 11

Oey Soe Tjoen 30
Oiling 25
Organizations 151–55
Origins 11
Overdyeing 85

Pangon, Madame 15
Paper 126
Paraffin wax 27, 49–51
Parang 36, 37
Patchy dyeing 70, 82
Pekalongan 30–3, 38
Perkin, William Henry 63
Pipette 131
Polychrome batik 29
Potassium permanganate 72
Pretreatment of fabric 25, 49, 65
Primary colour 59

Primissima 25
Procion dyes 64–7
    colour range 64
    recipe 65
    procedure 65, 87–91

Raffles, Sir Thomas 13
Ratio, dye bath 64
Rayon 46
Reactive dye preparation 88–91
Recipes, wax 51
Resin 24, 27, 49–53
Resist salt L 65
Rewaxing 113
Rice paste resist 19–23
Roketsu-zome 22

Safety precautions 45, 53, 74
Salt preparation 89
Salt crystal 131
Scales 60
Scraping off wax 30
Scouring 49
Sculpture 127
Sgraffito 121–2
Silk 47–8
Silk dyeing
    acid 72
    basic 72
    direct 71
    naphthol 70
    reactive 66
    vat 71
Silk painting 19–20, 115, 130–32
Silk route 11
Skill with canting 53–5
Slendang 25, 40
Sodium bicarbonate 66
Sodium silicate 66
Soga kerokan method 29–30
Speé, Miep 137
Spot removal 128
Spray dye 59, 77
Stamp printing 33–7, 123–4
Starszakowna, Norma 137–9

Steaming 74
Stencilling 76, 117, 125
Stipple wax 118–20, 136
Studio 45
Sumi brush 101
Surakarta 28
Switzerland 15

Thickener 66
Traditional patterns 37–41
Transferring designs 82
Tsutsugaki 20
Turkey red oil 68, 104
Tulis 12

Urea 66

Wax
    beeswax 27, 49–51
    biron 29–30
    klowong 29–30
    microcrystalline 27, 49–51
    paraffin 27, 49
    ready-made mixture 51
    recipes 50
    resin 51
    temperature 53
Wax procedures
    boiling out 30, 33, 111
    etching 120–1
    rewaxing 128–9
    scraping off 30
    spot removal 128
    stipple 118
Wax pot 53, 86
Wax printing 33–5, 123–4
Wax removal 79, 96–7, 128, 111
Wax texture effects 124, 126

Yahya, Amri 140–1
Yogyakarta 28
Yoruba tribe 17
Yusen 23

Zuylen, Eliza Van 11